Marketing Strategies

for the home-based business second edition

Shirley George Frazier

gpp®

Guilford, Connecticut

Interior spot art licensed by Shutterstock.com

Editorial Director: Cynthia Hughes Cullen
Editor: Tracee Williams
Project Editor: Lauren Brancato
Text Design: Sheryl P. Kober
Layout: Justin Marciano

ISBN 978-0-7627-8661-9

Printed in the United States of America
10 9 8 7 6 5 4 3 2 1

To my mom, daughter Genesis, and sister Cassandra,
who support my dreams, and to solo business owners worldwide
who toil endlessly and accomplish masterfully.

Contents

Introduction

There you are, leaving the house to walk your twin Yorkshire terriers or completing a clinical trial on stem cell research, when suddenly a life-changing business idea enters your head. The concept borders on brilliant, and it's a perfect platform to launch as a solo enterprise maintained at home.

You can see people of all ages or companies with large or small staffs buying the program and subscribing to additional services to successfully operate it. Your bank account grows—first by thousands and then hundreds of thousands—until you reach the one million dollar mark and more.

Life is poised to be a bed of roses. However, there's one detail to address that connects you with success. That detail is marketing. It's the part that wasn't conceived in the initial idea.

Marketing, as defined by the American Marketing Association (www .marketingpower.com), is "the activity, set of institutions, and processes for creating, communicating, delivering, and exchanging offerings that have value for customers, clients, partners, and society at large." That's the general definition. Marketing means much more to you, a person who invests a substantial amount of money in her own business. Marketing is:

- The main ingredient that commits your passion to paper, ensuring long-term success through economic and competitive changes.
- The important, behind-the-scenes work performed on a daily basis to make the dream a reality.
- A review of problems and pitfalls associated with why the idea may not launch according to schedule, and solutions that make those problems disappear.
- A mandatory activity that all aspiring and current business owners must perform but many neglect, which is a common reason why businesses close early in their life cycle.

Marketing isn't just for large corporations. The speed at which some big firms close shop proves that their marketing failed because it wasn't a primary detail in the initial planning stages. All the layers of management couldn't devise one workable plan for success.

Things will be different for you. There's just one layer in your organization. You are the person who sets the groundwork and implements the strategy that puts the product or service into the hands of individuals and/or businesses that need it most.

Your marketing plan starts with this book. Within these covers you will learn the techniques to successfully market in your backyard and around the world twenty-four hours a day, seven days a week.

This book contains many realistic methods that you, a dynamic new or seasoned solo business owner, can complete on your own or easily delegate to an intern or other type of helper (we'll discuss in this book how to get affordable help). However, no reference source helps if you are not committed to positive action. For example, a plan to contact a television producer to book an appearance is no good without the physical action of picking up the telephone and making the call or connecting with the producer through social media. If you're ready to be proactive, this is the resource that gets the ball rolling.

How I Got My Start

No one, including me, is born thinking that marketing will be their strength. It's only when you decide to start a business that research about your chosen industry allows the dots to finally connect. Those dots took root for my business from 1990 to 1995. In that time I developed and launched a marketing plan that was full of risk and ulti-mately successful. The results convinced gift industry trade show producers to invite me to speak about marketing at their events in New York City, Los Angeles, Chicago, Dallas, and more locations, including a show in Washington, DC. Five years earlier I entered that same show as an attendee, knowing little more about business than could fill a thimble. I recall walking up and down the trade show's aisles looking at everything from stationery to furniture. It was a dizzying experience.

I stopped to eat at the food court and went to a table occupied by two women. We introduced ourselves and traded business cards. The women were based in Virginia and, like me, were starting a business. One of them asked me, "What's your marketing plan?" I remember mentioning postcard mailings and word-of-mouth promotion, but my game plan barely existed. The options at that time seemed limited for a home-based owner. How was I to let people know I existed, and how would I position my products as items that attract and benefit individuals and corporations? These and other questions played over and over in my head during the train ride home.

Months after attending the show, I consulted library books and newsstand magazines. I attended small business seminars and enrolled in adult school courses. I read success stories about people who started businesses with a little or lots of cash. After listing on paper every conceivable way to market, I created a plan to make as much "noise" as possible at local events and through print and broadcast media, steadily adding more marketing ideas until the time was right for each one's implementation.

The plan began paying off, and success was steady. Photographs appeared in local newspapers, interviews and articles written by me emerged in business journals and magazines, advertisements played on radio stations, and my guest appearances increased on TV and cable shows. Colleagues around the country saw my name in so many places they asked if I had hired a publicist. I responded humbly without divulging my plan. On that cold train ride home from Washington to New Jersey, knowing that marketing was going to be a challenge, I decided to find clients through as many marketing opportunities available to me as possible. Convincing other people to share my vision was another part of the plan. For example, my mother willingly sat in my car, illegally parked between two trucks on New York City's Sixth Avenue, while I went into a building to deliver a marketing package to secure an appearance on the Food Network. That's one example of taking chances when your passion for business overwhelms sensibility. I'm not advocating that you break laws, but I am saying that your business life sits squarely in your hands. Sometimes you have to move forward even if you think you'll look out of place or be rejected. That's how marketing generates interest, excitement, and sales.

The last thing I want to do is paint a rosy picture of how everything falls into place when you start marketing. In many cases telephone calls and e-mail queries won't be returned. Someone else will get the cover story. Another person will be quoted instead of you, or you'll be misquoted. The person you follow on Twitter won't follow you back. You'll get upset and maybe shed tears. Some opportunities won't work out, and you'll be glad that others fell apart.

Now it's time for your marketing train to leave the station, destined for opportunities that take you to the top of your industry. Many lessons are about to be learned, and soon you may be just like me, turning your knowledge into a profitable way to put your marketing ideas in the fast lane.

Solo Business Statistics

You are an independent business person; however, you are not alone in creating and launching a successful enterprise with a dynamic marketing program as its foundation. According to the 2008 US Census (www.census.gov), 21.4 million independent business owners exist with combined revenues of $963 billion, and there are millions more operating businesses outside of the US. The word "independent," according to census reports, is defined as a company with no employees.

These are the top-ten independent industries, listed in order of revenue:

1. Real estate, renting, and leasing: $163 billion
2. Construction: $144 billion
3. Professional, scientific, and technical services: $132 billion
4. Retail trade: $84 billion
5. General services, too small to separate by category: $81 billion
6. Transportation and warehousing: $67 billion
7. Health care and social assistance: $58 billion
8. Finance and insurance: $56 billion
9. Administrative support, and waste management and remedial services: $40 billion
10. Wholesale trade: $36 billion

Don't be alarmed if your company's activities fall outside of this list. Many firms in industries large and small, with and without employees, reap the rewards of creating, launching, and monitoring marketing strategies that keep their businesses strong and successful.

How This Book Is Organized

You hold in your hands the source to dozens of strategies to market products and services. The number of options may overwhelm you. My mission is to expose all of the available tools and help you streamline your plan to accomplish the tasks that are manageable by you and any help you contract on a temporary basis from outside sources. It is important to create an organized marketing campaign that you can complete, control, and maintain. That's why this book takes you step-by-step to build your plan.

The first chapter explains all about marketing through the eyes of two business owners. One owns a new firm, and the other operates a mature business. Both require marketing support, but the way in which they focus on opportunities is quite different. The sample marketing plans in this chapter illustrate how to integrate separate tasks into one cohesive project and let you see what's possible for your business. A marketing plan will help you focus on your business passion and talent for telling the world your product or service is the next best thing to the iPad. In addition, the plans introduce you to concepts that we'll discuss in greater detail throughout the book.

After the marketing plan introduction, we'll turn our attention to the nuts and bolts of marketing: what's available, how much it costs, problems that may arise, and results you can realistically achieve. Chapters 2 and 3 prepare you to spread your business message in social media and professional settings, as well as to create and distribute promotional items that convince customers to purchase what you sell.

Getting the media on your publicity bandwagon is the focus of chapters 4 and 5. Whether you seek validation in print or are ready for a televised close-up, these chapters educate you about the process and point you in the right direction.

Home-based business owners cannot prosper without an Internet presence to complement social media, and that's why chapters 6 and 7 are dedicated to maximizing your reach on the web. When it's time to set up your website or blog, distribute electronic newsletters, create videos, spread your message through social media, and get help to put and keep it all together running like a well-oiled machine, you'll be prepared after reading these chapters.

After all of your hard work, the last thing you need is to have your competitors take the marketing techniques you create and put their names on it. That's why security issues are discussed in chapter 8. Knowing how to protect your work is especially helpful when creating marketing products that double as intellectual property, a priceless commodity for today's solo business owner.

Chapter 9 helps you decide what types of gifts to buy for loyal customers and where to find these incentive products that keep customers happy and business profitable. This chapter is a must if you appreciate devoted clients and the referral business gained from their online and word-of-mouth promotions.

The real-life marketing examples throughout this book prove that the phrase "What can happen will happen" is alive and well. Chapter 10 features stories from independent marketers who share challenges and the steps taken to find solutions. At the end, you'll know how to decide which marketing strategies are for you and which are not yet beneficial for your business.

Caveats to Consider as You Start

As you begin the marketing process, let me reveal some dos and don'ts to keep in mind

Do:

- Keep pen and paper, smartphone, or tablet by your side as you read this book to jot down ideas at a moment's notice.
- Encourage potential buyers to share their insights about the products and services you sell or plan to sell. Listen to their ideas and incorporate the possibilities. Do not let negative thoughts expressed by others derail your plans (see the list of don'ts for more on this).
- Plan on adding social media as part of your overall marketing strategy. You'll be amazed at how far your message travels to reach a worldwide audience.
- Read news materials to learn how other companies market what they sell and the problems and solutions associated with promotion.
- Measure results of your marketing campaigns to understand what works, which areas need more attention, and which ones to eliminate.

Don't:

- Allow fear or procrastination to paralyze you. Mistakes will be made, and each will teach you lessons while moving you closer to smarter or alternative marketing decisions or results.
- Believe that six months of marketing translates into big profits. It will take more time and patience to get your promotional train on track.
- Allow negativity from outside sources to derail your plans. Let your instincts lead you down the path that you believe is best for business.
- Use a buckshot approach when launching plans. In many cases it's wise to

test your campaign on a small segment of a larger group. The results help you to fix any problems before distributing the message to a wider audience.

■ Attempt to accomplish every marketing idea simultaneously. Choose options that make the most sense, incorporating other ideas when the time is right.

When properly performed, marketing ensures that your business gets noticed online and offline by prospects, clients, the media, and competitors. It leads to your ultimate goal—sales and more marketing opportunities from interested parties who find you through multiple marketing channels.

Defining a marketing channel:
http://thelawdictionary.org/marketing-channel

If you're ready to start, turn the page and let's begin.

01 Your Marketing Plan—The First Step to Success

One of the most difficult processes, outside of the physical work required to put your goals in play, is to create a marketing plan. This chapter introduces you to marketing plan basics.

You may have heard of great plans conceived on napkins, during train rides, or in the shower. All of this is probably true, but where the plan was created isn't important. What is crucial is documenting your ideas with pen and paper, in a marketing plan software program, or by typing and saving it in your computer. From there, the plan is fashioned into logical order so it moves from concept to execution.

The marketing plan is a written strategy created by you. It defines how to mold your idea into a full-fledged, revenue-earning business. You may decide to show the plan to trusted advisers who can provide advice and guidance and to investors with money to fund your venture.

Most home-based and solo business owners want to leapfrog this process and simply start the business. Neglecting to put your marketing plan on paper, however, is a misstep that causes chaos and catastrophes for business owners. Some survive, and others promptly go out of business.

If success means anything to you, then it makes sense that the plan to market a business and keep it thriving is worth time and effort. Your long-term success depends on it.

This chapter contains two marketing plans. One focuses on a product-based business, and the other maps the strategy for a service-based firm. Your company will fall into one of these categories even if you are web-based. Carefully review each firm's goals and objectives. References to both companies and their owners will appear throughout the book so you experience their choices and can better determine how you will make decisions based on marketing options in your own business.

Marketing Plan No. 1: Product Business

Roger Green owns Teed Up, a golf equipment and sports training firm based in Charlotte, North Carolina. Teed Up helps the general public get acquainted with golf and equips players at every level of experience with tools and support. The company informs customers about the latest products to increase their accuracy and also provides a learning experience to enjoy the game.

Teed Up's golf products are mainly sold online, while services that bring attention and sales to the product line are provided by Roger. The ancillary services that Roger offers help to raise awareness about his products and their availability on request or through the online store.

The company will officially open in six months, and Roger plans to begin marketing the business locally. He hopes to branch out his promotion statewide through a series of sponsorships, targeted mailings, social media, and electronic newsletters all tied together through his forthcoming website.

Roger knows that the golf industry is rife with local suppliers, online competitors, and specialty magazines. He especially understands that his one-man operation will need support on occasion from temporary workers and virtual assistants, but he believes that by marketing within the local area, he can succeed at winning business and gaining loyalty over time. Here's how Roger plans to market.

Sample Marketing Plan No. 1

Teed Up

Charlotte, North Carolina

Roger Green, Owner

Marketing Plan

2013

Company Mission

Market Statistics

Sports Outlook

Marketing Goals

Year 1 Objectives

Web Strategy

Golf Course Alliances

Other Marketing Options

Potential Problems and Solutions

Year 5 Objectives

Company Mission

Teed Up supplies equipment, training materials, and support to adults and youth at all skill levels who wish to learn and enjoy golf and want the experience to be memorable, successful, and fun.

Market Statistics

- Target Market

- Adults ages 18–55, youths ages 4–17

- Target Region

- Teed Up targets the sixteen counties of the Charlotte metropolitan area.

Regional Statistics

According to the Charlotte Chamber of Commerce's 2011 figures, the region boasts 1.6 million residents, with an annual growth rate of 3.6 percent per year. There is a total of 306,500 households, of which 44.7 percent have a buying income of at least $50,000.

Population by age as of 2011 breaks down as follows:

- Age 50 and older—53.9 percent

- Ages 35–49—24.5 percent

- Ages 25–34—16.9 percent

- Ages 18–24—8.8 percent

- Age 17 and younger—25.9 percent

Large businesses in the Charlotte area total 894, according to the chamber. The top-five industries are:

- Printing—140

- Machinery—95

- Chemical—64

- Furniture—47

- Food manufacturing—40

Business information is crucial to my success as Teed Up moves toward partnerships and sponsorships between Year 1 and Year 5.

Sports Outlook
Nongolf Sports

The chamber of commerce brands Charlotte as a "national sports hub." The region plays host to a men's and a women's basketball franchise, a motor speedway, professional football and soccer teams, and minor league baseball and hockey affiliates.

Golf

Charlotte is home to eighty golf courses, two of which are listed in *Golf Digest* as top US courses. The Professional Golf Association's Wells Fargo championship is played here each May, and other PGA tournaments are located in adjacent states.

Marketing Goals
Year 1

To introduce and sell products and services to 1) area residents who actively participate in sports activities, and 2) independent business owners and company executives who golf to network and secure business.

Year 5

To build long-term partnerships with local residents, regional businesses, and state-wide sports teams, leading to sales from and sponsorships with each segment.

Year 1 Objectives

Adult Market

Golf and other sports are a welcome part of Charlotte's culture. The question here is not how to get adults interested in the sport but rather "How do I create a long-term bond of trust and support to make the name 'Teed Up' synonymous with fun on a personal level and rewarding on a business level?" The answer is threefold: benefits, repetition, and nonsports (business and cultural community) memberships and sponsorships.

Benefits. While conducting informal surveys, I discovered one central theme echoed by adults who golf and those who want to participate: Local golf suppliers do not provide ongoing support to adults who spend thousands of dollars purchasing equipment and supplies.

Along with general marketing to introduce my business and the benefits I provide to clients who enjoy golf during practice and tournament play, I will focus on marketing my postsale support so that adults do not feel abandoned after spending any level of money on tools and equipment. This will be done through postsale contact by phone and e-mail, through mailed postcards with tips, through instructional updates on the company website and YouTube channel, through Teed Up's Twitter account and Facebook page, and by offering free thirty-minute in-person tutorials for individuals spending $1,500 or more. A low-cost "How to Enjoy Golf" e-book will be published as part of the business launch, and a Pinterest account is to be established to share photographs of new golf products and supplies of interest to adults and youth along with links leading to the website and the company's other online marketing channels.

Repetition. A mailing list will be created with names, addresses, and other personal and sports-related information. I plan to mail quarterly postcards and publish a monthly online newsletter to these contacts, and both will include calls to action encouraging recipients to visit specific pages on the website. The time line will be monitored and changed as needed.

Mailings using these two formats work to keep Teed Up in clients' minds whenever they're ready to learn about new golf products and schedule instructional support. In addition, anyone with school-aged children may see the Teed Up name in school newsletters and on school grounds as we pursue a relationship with the Charlotte Board of Education.

Nonsports memberships/sponsorships. Introducing and keeping Teed Up's name front and center is the goal. That's why it's important to become involved in events that are based on business and social community activities.

This includes memberships and sponsorships at chamber of commerce events, summer concert series, museum galas, sporting events, and other gatherings that attract individuals and organizations made up of people who golf or have strong potential to make golf part of their lives.

My calendar already includes a list of events that I will attend, from which I will decide which gatherings are worth pursuing for partnerships on a member or sponsorship basis.

Adult Marketing—Custom Services

Teed Up plans to duplicate the same customer service traits as the tie industry by taking golf clubs, shoes, and accessories to businessmen and women within the corporate sector. Offering an "on the road, one-stop shop" at corporate facilities is a convenience that will win many clients.

I have purchased three cases to hold tees, balls, caps, clubs, and other products that golfers frequently request as well as new innovations they may not know exist. These cases sit on top of a cart that easily travels in my vehicle and into office buildings. Clients will be able to see what's available in three ways:

1. I will call prospects who are the best targets for selling within offices. Meetings (a better word than "appointments") will be pursued by phone and customized newsletter, and I will market the supplies to prospects during business hours.

2. Customers can schedule meetings through a link on my website. Once the meeting request is received, I will e-mail a confirmation and confirm again the day before the meeting.
3. Clients can call Teed Up directly to schedule a meeting to see new and popular products. Again, I will arrive at their office during business hours to show them requested items and other accessories they may not have considered buying.

This service will be marketed as a time-saver, eliminating the need for clients to drive out of their way to a retail store. Sales are possible not only through the targeted clients but also through associates in the office who golf or want to learn the sport.

Sales through each customized visit are estimated at $500 to $5,000, and orders will be processed during the meeting through a free smartphone app. In addition, information about my website, instructional service, youth mentorship program (for their children), and available products and accessories that are not on-site will be discussed before the meeting's conclusion.

Youth Market

Charlotte's educational system, the twenty-third largest district in the United States, contains 150 schools educating 126,903 students in grades pre-K to 12.

Studies have shown that there is a direct correlation between high achievement in school and the discipline students learn through sports participation. Teed Up plans to speak with board of education administrators and teachers to introduce a golf training program for students enrolled in grades 4 through 12.

My first step is to research golf programs in school districts throughout the United States to assist me in creating a program for this area (no program exists to date). In addition, I will enlist the help of virtual assistants to call golf centers that have developed these programs to ask questions not answered on their websites and to uncover problems associated with program implementation. This will allow me to prepare what-if scenarios that educators will expect me to address.

Finally, this project will begin as a pilot program within three grades—4, 7, and 10—at two of the district's smaller schools. I will test, develop, and refine the project before recruiting outside assistance as Teed Up expands to work with additional grades.

I plan to contact golf product manufacturers to cosponsor the program with supplies for participating students.

Working with students will help me to accomplish three goals.

1. Secure a lifelong relationship with youngsters as they continue playing golf as adults.
2. Work with parents who, through their children, become enamored with the sport.
3. Brand my company as it becomes aligned with the community, region, and state.

Web Strategy

A website URL, host company, shopping cart, and credit card acceptance is in place. The hosting firm's yearly fee is $96, a low investment that allows me to put my marketing dollars into other categories.

Teed Up has retained the services of a college intern at a cost of $15 per hour who will create the company website. The estimated total cost is $500 for the initial site, after which I will take over the monthly maintenance until one of the virtual assistants working on another project proves to be adept at website updates.

The site will contain a mix of information for beginner to advanced players, plus sections for adults and children who have an interest in golf, need to refresh their knowledge after a winter break, or require guidance as they become more proficient.

I visualize the following for the website:

Home page. The main page will welcome visitors with images of golfers of various ages and in a variety of settings. Photographs added to the home page and other pages on the site will be posted from authorized online image banks, and videos hosted by Teed Up's YouTube channel will display demonstration techniques featuring guidance by me to adults and students.

Equipment page. Shown on this page is a breakdown of the basic supplies and tools required to play golf. This page will lead to subpages according to age, gender, and skill level. It will also include links to my online shopping cart.

Wardrobe page. Sports-related clothing is an important part of golf. This page will keep visitors informed about fashion trends for all ages and genders as well as provide links to clothing suppliers chosen for their trend-setting styles and Teed Up's ability to partner with them as affiliates.

Frequently asked questions (FAQ) page. Basic questions and answers to general and complex golfing questions are here. This section will be segmented according to topic, such as clubs, etiquette, rules, etc. I anticipate that this area will expand over time and become an important resource to area residents, cementing Teed Up's reputation as a community knowledge bank.

Calendar page. This is a list of instruction schedules and upcoming events planned throughout the Charlotte area in which Teed Up will participate and/or sponsor.

Links page. This area includes website links to area golf courses, national magazines, tournament scores, Teed Up's video and social media pages, and noncompetitive golf-related sites.

"About us" page. Featured here are insights into the company, my golf background, list of clients, and roster of publicity gained through broadcast, social media, and print exposure.

Comments page. Clients who provide their insights and experience about our products and services will have their comments in print and video posted here. This is also the area where visitors can include their comments as well as ask questions about the site.

Social media. I will dispense a variety of golf tips, promotional photos, videos, and sponsorship notices through the Twitter account, Facebook and Pinterest pages, YouTube channel, and blog, all created to complement my website. [Note: Social media is explained in chapter 2.]

Golf Course Alliances

There are many opportunities to work with the area's eighty golf courses, so I plan to start slowly and tactfully to create alliances that do not injure my association with the courses that bring me the most business.

My plan is to work with five courses of varying size that cater to different segments of the Charlotte community. I cannot compete with the on-site pro, nor do I wish to, but I can act as an outside resource when the resident pro is in a position to recommend ancillary services.

Meeting selected golf pros for lunch one at a time will put the two of us in a casual setting to discuss the options available for partnerships. During the meal I will ask questions to learn more about:

1. Client characteristics at each facility.
2. Future plans for course upgrades and expansion.
3. Changes that each pro sees occurring locally and in the overall industry.
4. How we can team up in the future for collaborations online and at their respective facilities.

These answers will help me to understand how to market Teed Up within the region, to golf course management, and to individual adults outside of the facility.

Other Marketing Options

Five more ideas worth pursuing are:

1. Speaking at business and social functions on how golf creates stronger relationships.
2. Creating an e-book (as mentioned earlier) with golf strategies and basic rules of the game.
3. Writing golf articles for submission to Charlotte and North Carolina publications.
4. Contacting area television and radio shows to learn how to schedule a segment to share golf tips with viewers and listeners.
5. Sponsoring youth tournaments and awarding winners with lessons and equipment.

My virtual assistant will help coordinate this schedule.

Potential Problems and Solutions

Teed Up must be willing and able to make adjustments to this marketing plan if some goals are not achievable. Listed here are areas that may require changes.

Problem: Charlotte's board of education is not agreeable to creating a youth program.

Solution: Work directly with parents who want their children introduced to the sport.

Problem: Meeting with corporate clients at their offices does not net the anticipated sales level per meeting.

Solution: Create an incentive program to encourage additional sales and referral business.

Problem: The website's host suddenly ceases business, leaving Teed Up without a web presence.

Solution: Make sure the website is backed up on my own computer and also through an online or offline external backup program. Then search for another, more reliable host and upload my site to its server.

Year 5 Objectives

By 2018 my roots will be firmly planted in Charlotte's golf communities due to the accomplishments achieved in the first five years.

Plans during this stage are to:

1. Assess which activities are bringing the most recognition and sales. Reduce or eliminate lower sales activities.
2. Create a golf school cosponsored by industry manufacturers.
3. Secure a position as a board of director at one of the local golf associations.

These and more plans will be developed and refined as Year 5 approaches.

Marketing Plan No. 2: Service Business

Janet Ross is a certified public accountant (CPA) and owner of AccountAble, an accounting firm based in Denver, Colorado. This is Janet's sixth year in business. Her office is located at home in a den converted into an office. It's a room that has a separate door as an entrance, which makes it easy for clients to visit her if she is unable to go to their home or office.

The start-up phase was busy and profitable as Janet honed her skills at making contact with small and large businesses that became clients. She was able to retain a few jobs from larger CPA firms that recommended her services to small and solo business owners who could not afford the larger companies' fees.

The region's business climate is changing, and Janet knows this by the decreasing size of her clientele. Companies in the area have relocated or consolidated, and the emergence of online and big box retailers has forced some of Janet's clients to go out of business.

It's a situation that Janet dreads, and although she's seen the changes over the past two years, Janet did not take the time to review her marketing plan to decide how to keep her client roster and sales increasing through the change. Janet is experiencing a common hazard of being in business for yourself. You hope that things will stay the same, but they rarely do.

The city's economic development department reports that new companies are considering relocation to the area, but Janet cannot wait for these firms to make their decisions. She needs to revise her marketing plan now if she is to survive through regional changes that occur in the future.

One service that Janet does not offer is financial planning. It's a comfortable offshoot to her accounting work that has the potential to bolster and rebrand her firm.

A second service is information sharing through speaking engagements. There are many possibilities for teaming up with banking institutions and city groups, but before Janet pursues this, she must overcome her fear of speaking. Although passionate about her work, stage fright has kept her away from the podium. Janet knows that to make potential customers comfortable with her ability, she'll have to get rid of her jitters and start speaking on a regular basis.

A third area for boosting business is adding more promotional materials available in print and on her website to her roster, materials that are filled with financial planning tips and other ideas that help her clients keep more money in their pockets. Janet knows that outsourcing firms exist to prepare these important mailing pieces, which she will send to clients at least once per quarter.

Janet wonders why she hadn't considered all of this two years ago, but she won't dwell on the past. It's time to make sure that the sixth and forthcoming years in business are as profitable, if not more so, as the first five. Here's what Janet plans to keep her business thriving.

Sample Marketing Plan No. 2

AccountAble
Denver, Colorado
Janet Ross, CPA–Owner
Marketing Plan
2013

Company mission—Year 1
Current mission—Year 5
Business outlook
Client base
Marketing options
Blog Site establishment
Other options
Marketing timetable
Wrap up

Company Mission—Year 1
To provide accounting help to individuals and small business owners who cannot or do not have time to prepare their own income taxes and other tax documents.

Current Mission—Year 5
To 1) provide accounting and financial planning services to high-income individuals, and 2) make my services available to large, local accounting firms that outsource work assigned to them by smaller clients.

Business Outlook

My firm thrived between 2007 and 2010. Sales grew at a rate of 12 percent a year thanks to establishing relationships at networking events; work assigned to me by colleagues relocating to other areas; and referrals made by small business clients to colleagues who were starting a business, who were unsatisfied with their accountant, or who decided to focus on their main work rather than keep track of their financials.

The economic climate has changed dramatically in the last two years (only 5 percent growth combined in 2011 and 2012, versus 12 percent from 2007 to 2010). I must now look at the big picture to determine how my company will survive as clients decrease due to consolidations, closings, and relocations.

Client Base

My current client roster includes:

1. Four retail businesses (furniture store, flower shop, tuxedo rental, and independent party store)
2. Three service businesses (concrete mixer, chain of launderettes, and landscaper)
3. Two wholesalers (handbag manufacturer and food broker)

This is approximately half of the business I normally serviced throughout the previous five years. Although business has increased from the remaining firms, there is no guarantee that these companies will stay in business or once again contract my services.

I will continue to provide diligent service to my customers, promoting the new financial services that focus on keeping more money in their pockets.

Other avenues will be pursued to grow my business yet keep within manageable bounds as a solo business proprietor. Considerations are explained within this plan.

Marketing Options
New Opportunity—Speaking Engagements

I envy individuals who can present their topics to audiences small and large. If my business is to thrive, I will have to join this enviable group.

The first step is to decide how to translate my industry knowledge into information that the general public understands and in a way that keeps them listening. Hearing other speakers has taught me that I must balance industry insights with real-life events and humorous stories, all based around accounting and finance. That will not be difficult because of what I've learned and heard from other accountants. The difficult part will be reducing my speaking jitters.

One of my clients, a handbag manufacturer who speaks at trade shows, works with a coach that I will contact for assistance. Her website information already has me feeling more at ease. I'm nervous but looking forward to working on this weakness and adding speaking engagements to my list of marketing methods.

New Service—Profit Mentoring

Financial planning will be added to my core services. It's an area that I've considered for several years but was too busy to develop. Because I'm aware of clients' tax situations, offering planning help is a natural progression to add to assure my firm's longevity.

Word-of-mouth marketing will be used diligently each time I meet with clients at my office or at their location. I can talk about planning strategies in terms of each client's specific situation and how my services will help increase their business revenue and personal income. Easy-to-understand articles available in brochure form will be ready to distribute in a few months (those brochures will also point to more information and profit calculators on my website), which I will carry with me to give to clients after informing them about my additional service. Everyone wants to know how to keep more of the money he or she earns. My pitch will focus on this goal.

New Service—Brochure Distribution

Past methods of distributing information about my firm included a regular-size sheet of paper with my business name at the top and details about my services and rates. Today's clientele expects, and rightfully so, to receive something more professional and accessible online.

Thank goodness there are companies who specialize in creating brochures and pamphlets for accountants. These firms make general materials available, customized with the accounting firm's name. They also provide mailing services. At the least a brochure keeps clients aware of my service, and at most it can be passed on to associates who read the tips and see my name on the material. This can lead to additional clients or at least to telephone calls, e-mails from prospects, or an increase in website visits.

Two West Coast companies create these customized materials for accounting professionals who don't have time to make their own. After reviewing their websites, I will contact them for samples and rates. I'll also contact industry colleagues to learn what type of marketing information they distribute online. Then I will decide which firm is my best option and begin working with them, monitoring the results to see whether or not business stays stable or if added profits occur due to this investment.

Accounting Firm Collaborations

Previous dealings with larger area accounting firms resulted in assignments during their peak seasons, which often occurs when my workload is not as stringent. This additional business has blossomed because of relationships created with other accountants at CPA association conferences.

Starting this year I plan to aggressively pursue this type of work. Here are the steps I will take to get more business.

- Call my past contacts to initiate conversations to uncover opportunities for outsourced work in the future.

- Advertise my accounting specialties in the local chamber of commerce publication and state accounting magazine. This strategy will cost $200 and $400 per printing, respectively, for a four-inch ad.

- Pursue a feature story in the local newspaper on how small businesses serve the needs of larger firms. The feature-story editor and I are members of the same women's group. She may be interested in this type of article, which will serve to promote my services to firms that read the newspaper in print or online.

The opportunity to work with larger accounting firms may be closed because of internal consolidations, but such consolidation might make this a viable option because of fewer accountants on their payrolls. In either case, making more accounting firms aware of my presence and abilities will open the door to new relationships.

Blog Site Establishment

My main focus has been on maintaining a solid roster of clients who contract my accounting services throughout the year. The Internet was not part of my planning, but adding a blog to market my services has the potential to help me secure new clients.

The office is equipped with Internet access, and with that I've decided that a blog is better for my business than a website. I'm a better writer than speaker, and research reveals that while websites and blogs are both popular, weekly blog updates may be friendlier for search engine optimization (SEO is explained in chapter 7). In addition, I require a software program to host the blog as well as social media programs to market my expertise online.

At a recent networking meeting, I spoke with a woman who is a trusted resource on Internet practices. She provided me with several website addresses that educate new bloggers on how to establish a presence through traditional marketing and social media.

This expert agreed to help me establish a blog, including securing my business name as the online domain name. I will provide her with information for blog creation. The initial material, developed after reviewing the few accounting-based blogs available from other financial specialists, includes:

1. Basic information about my firm and the types of businesses that depend on my service
2. My industry experience and a roster of current clients
3. A list of IRS calendar schedules and timetables for tax completion
4. Year-round tips to help visitors prepare for tax time
5. A page explaining why individuals and businesses hire me to keep them financially on track, and various options to contact me

6. Articles that provide basic information on taxes and finances, tips that piggyback on current trends, and rebuttals to misinformation printed on other sites and blogs

This blog and all the necessities to get it up and running will cost approximately $500, a worthwhile investment that will deliver additional business in the long run. It will certainly help clients and prospects become aware of my services, whether they are currently in town or moving to this area.

Other Options

Self-imposed brainstorming sessions conducted in the past two weeks have developed the following ideas for further consideration:

1. Donate no more than three one-hour accounting consultations at the next black-tie charity.
2. Purchase customized travel logs for distribution to customers who drive their personal cars for business purposes.
3. Create an association of service professionals who learn from each other and recommend each other's services to their respective clients.
4. Conduct a specialized accounting/financial class through a local adult school for product and service-based business owners.
5. Distribute an online newsletter that complements the print edition when my blog is operational.
6. Develop and launch an online radio show as I manage my fear of public speaking (web radio is discussed in chapter 6).

Marketing Timetable
Public Speaking Support

- Make contact with speaking coach: this month (March).

- Work with coach to reduce speaking anxiety: three months (May to July).

- Create a roster of three financial seminars of forty-five minutes each: two months (June and July).

- Call a maximum of six groups to book speaking engagements: throughout March. (Calls must be made early in the year due to each group's booking schedules.)

- Secure first speaking opportunity: between September 2013 and January 2014.

- Launch my online radio show as the coaching sessions progress (May/June).

Profit Mentoring

- Decide on the specialty financial areas I will offer (SEP retirement funds, employee profit sharing, etc.): first quarter.

- Review clients' files to determine services each needs most: first quarter.

- Alert clients to new mentoring program: ongoing through the year.

- Create brochures with mentoring information: first or second quarter (see "Brochure Distribution"). If the brochures are ready within the second quarter, they can be distributed to prospects and clients as a follow-up to the mentoring sessions.

Brochure Distribution

- Request brochure samples from printers: first quarter.

- Speak with colleagues regarding their distribution sources: January and February.

- Determine which brochures are best for marketing purposes: first quarter.

- Make sure brochures can include my blog address and social media links: first quarter.

- Order brochures: second quarter.

- Determine which brochures look best to raise business awareness: ongoing.

Note: Brochure order must be timed with securing blog and social media accounts (see info under "Blog Site Establishment").

Accounting Firm Collaborations

- Contact firms that have provided me with past work: ongoing.

- Contact colleagues at additional firms whom I have met at industry meetings and other gatherings: January and February and from May onward.

- Determine which opportunities are likely and pursue potential business and collaborative work: ongoing; review each month.

- Secure advertising with trade magazines and the chamber of commerce newspaper to market general expertise and subcontracting experience: ASAP at yearly rate.

Media Promotion

- Contact feature-story editor with article idea: January, March, April, August, ongoing.

- Stay in touch with editor for other article ideas through her or news colleagues: ongoing.

Blog Site Establishment

- Review accounting-based blogs to determine and finalize my blog's details: first quarter.

- Set up appointment to meet with blog consultant and finalize project launch and completion dates as well as ongoing updates and monitoring: first or second quarter.

- Determine when blog domain name and blog host will be obtained: first quarter.

- Order new stationery and business cards that include blog and social media information: second quarter.

- Ensure that blog, e-mail, and social media information are added to brochures: see "Brochure Distribution" above.

Other Options

■ Review brainstorming ideas on a quarterly basis. Work on ideas that are ready for launch, add projects for consideration, and eliminate ideas that no longer fit the marketing plan.

Wrap Up

The sooner my plan is put into action, the better. Therefore, most of my goals will begin immediately and be completed by midyear. Timing plays a big part in this plan because of 1) the accounting period from January to April, 2) blog and social media launch plans, 3) the need to increase my client roster, and 4) the desire to create marketing materials that promote my financial planning expertise and online information.

Many of my plans focus around making telephone calls or requesting information by e-mail. I can review and approve requested materials before the workday begins and in the evening.

Creating Your Own Plan

Each of the marketing plans above has room to address additional options. Both provide the essential parts of a well-designed strategy. Your plan's elements depend on numerous factors, many of which are addressed by Teed Up and AccountAble. A well-rounded marketing plan includes:

Mission statement: The defining sentence that explains your business's focus.

Business overview: An honest look at what you plan to sell and why it's beneficial to the target market.

Target market: Facts related to potential buyers, including their characteristics, geographic location, and other supporting documentation.

Marketing goals: A list of actions that outlines how the plan will connect products and services with customers. This encompasses every opportunity in print, by word of mouth, through broadcast channels, and on the Internet.

Marketing objectives: A breakdown of steps to accomplish each goal.

Other goals for consideration: A list of additional marketing options. These are ideas that did not make the short list but are considerations for future implementation.

Financial aspects: A monetary breakdown of costs associated with each goal. Costs can be separated throughout the financial subsection or integrated within the goals' structure.

Timetable: A recap of all goals and objectives, matched with an overview of when each is scheduled for completion.

Plan B: No plan is foolproof, which means that problems and/or missteps are a consideration. List the likely problems and solutions to put in place at a moment's notice. A plan B strategy appears in the Teed Up marketing plan.

Review and Revisions

Create your own timetable to keep the marketing plan up to date and on schedule. A monthly review is recommended, but only you know what works for your business. Post a reminder system on your wall, desk calendar, electronic calendar, or marketing software system.

Stay on schedule. Your efforts will pay off, and marketing will become as habitual as waking each morning.

If you stop consulting the plan for a period of time, don't discard it completely. The best marketers occasionally get sidetracked. Pick up the plan, review it, make updates, and get your business back on track. As long as you're still in business, it's not too late to try again.

02 | Relationship Marketing, Solo-Style

What was once referred to in the business world as "networking" is frequently replaced by the word "relationship." It better expresses interaction between two people meeting for the first time and learning about each other's life-styles both within and outside of business. A bond forms, leading to more-frequent discussions. In time, if one person needs guidance or a reference, the other person obliges without hesitation. Relationships are the bridge that helps us entrepreneurs create strong businesses through alliances with other people. This chapter is your guide to build confidence so your relationships blossom into profitable opportunities.

Once you decide on your profession and its mission (all outlined within a business plan), the business name of your choosing is registered with the proper authorities in your city, state, or country. After that, you can set up your identity on the Internet to let everyone in your personal online circles know that you're in business.

We'll review how to market in person, but let's start with the easiest and still-free places online to launch your marketing. Even if you don't think you'll ever promote your business through these avenues, it's still a wise move to create accounts through the following programs to secure your identity (personal name and/or business name) before another person does so for unscrupulous reasons.

Online: Setting Up and Marketing Your Web Identity

Participating in online social media as part of your marketing strategy is a must in today's society. Customers will expect to find you on one or more of the following programs. Tips you find here for each social media account you create will encourage customers and visitors to connect with you and interact with other followers.

Facebook

Create a Facebook page for your business whether you've already established a personal page on Facebook or have skipped joining this popular program. The main set-up page guides you though choosing the correct structure (local, company, brand, etc.) and category before entering your company name in the appropriate box and establishing the page. These structures encourage people to "like" or follow the page, which is different than personal pages where people ask you, as an individual, to be mutual friends.

Creating your Facebook page: www.facebook.com/pages/create.php

---

Once set up, you can add an identifying picture (known as the header, which you can update as many times as you wish), company slogan or mission, location, website URL, and telephone number.

If you already have a personal Facebook page, invite people who are your Facebook friends to "like" your page. That will create your initial following. Clients and other people online who visit your website or blog will, in time, follow your page as you market it through free and fee-based tools that Facebook offers.

Populate the page every day, week, or month with information that excites and educates followers. It's advised that you share details as often as possible, at least once a day or three times a week at a minimum to promote the business and grow your following. Here's what you can include:

1. Pictures of customers with you and a capture stating why they are happy with the product.
2. Written testimonials from satisfied clients.
3. Announcements about contests and where on your website or blog to find details.
4. Questions that survey followers about their preferences related to your products.
5. A cartoon or another photograph of something humorous related to your product or an upcoming national event (G-rated humor can be a fun part of your page).

Include pictures with every page update. Followers appreciate seeing a visual image that accompanies the text message.

In time, you can outsource Facebook responsibilities to a virtual assistant or another support person. That's what Roger Green of Teed Up intends to do after he creates a monthly schedule of page updates.

Twitter

You'll find that some clients prefer Facebook because it's a source for images, while Twitter is where clients who prefer reading text messages migrate.

If you don't yet have a Twitter account, consider establishing one in your personal name rather than your business name. Doing this lets your Twitter followers know that they are reading messages from a person who shares informative tweets and links and not a business that advertises in every message.

> **Joining Twitter:** www.twitter.com

Once established on Twitter, you can decorate your account page with a background image supplied by Twitter or create a custom image that includes your picture, a company logo, or other details about your business. The account page will include recommendations for people to follow; however, it's your responsibility to find and follow interesting tweeters in your industry, in the media, and in your current business and personal circles.

Three points about your Twitter account:

1. Try, at the beginning, to only follow as many people as you can realistically monitor. Some Twitter users follow tens of thousands of people. While that may be fine for them because they are long-time Twitter participants, it may be better for you to start with no more than one hundred people on your follow list unless your profession forces you to add more.
2. Compliment another Twitter user if she was mentioned in the newspaper, performed a good deed, or spoke at an event you recently attended. Compliments often go viral, and that encourages more Twitter users to follow you, including the person you complimented.

3. Don't be offended if people you follow don't follow you back. Some will reciprocate while others won't. An interesting Twitter description about yourself and link to your site or blog will encourage people to follow you.

As with Facebook, updating your Twitter account can be given to a virtual assistant unless you plan to control tweeting messages and monitoring responses.

You'll find a story in chapter 10 on how an important connection came together through Twitter for a television appearance.

LinkedIn

If making connections with business people is your goal, then LinkedIn has an advantage over other social media. When launched, LinkedIn established itself as the place to "exchange knowledge, ideas, and opportunities with a broader network of professionals." Whether you want to find corporate business leads or find more competitors, LinkedIn is your source.

When joining LinkedIn, you can set up accounts as an individual and as a business. The latter wasn't available when the program launched; however, establishing your business identity here can expose your business to people in your target market.

Complete all information to create your personal and business profiles. Don't worry if you're not able to provide customer testimonials as part of your description. When you join LinkedIn and use its internal search engine to uncover colleagues and associates who are already there, request them to provide you with recommendations. A good way to do this is to write the comment for them according to successful past results. Present the comment to them and ask that they either copy and paste it as written within their LinkedIn account or edit the text before posting it. Be sure that your written recommendation genuinely and honestly promotes your business.

Setting up your LinkedIn account: www.linkedin.com

This site is different than other social media programs. You can ask questions where experts provide opinions and solutions, and members who ask questions can receive the same from you. You can also establish an industry group on LinkedIn and solicit members from businesses and customers already on the program. Already-established groups are usually open to join, though some owners review your account before approving your membership.

LinkedIn isn't as simple to navigate as Facebook and Twitter, which means there are many options for you to create strong bonds with local and international business owners. Make time in your schedule to review what's available and connect with interesting people worldwide.

YouTube

Just imagine—your recorded speeches, product demonstrations, customer and professional interviews—all residing in one place online where customers and other interested people can watch at any time. YouTube is the world's host for everything recorded in video format, and it's the place to promote your visual message.

Opening a YouTube account: www.youtube.com

People at industry events have encouraged me to host my videos at sites competitive to YouTube because "YouTube is crowded." While the web's second most-visited site (as of July 2011 according to Doubleclick.com) contains millions of videos, all of them do not feature your business or industry, so why not market here? Open an account, create a channel, upload videos, and invite your customers to subscribe and watch.

What's even better than having customers visit your YouTube channel is copying the recording code for each video that YouTube provides within your account (anyone can access the code to share your videos, which is important for marketing purposes) and paste the code into your website or blog so the video plays on your space. You-Tube also allows you to host private videos, which are viewed by people who receive each video's special URL directly from you.

Customizing Your YouTube Channel

You establish a YouTube channel when you open your account. Once you register on YouTube, a channel is created when you set up your account as your business name so visitors to your channel type www.youtube.com/yourchannelname to find your videos. You can customize the channel's home page with your business logo, URL, and other details.

This is how my videos are distributed on the web. Each video is recorded using a camcorder. It's then converted and uploaded to my business's YouTube channel. Subscribers watch it there or will see it on my website, blog, or another online space where the video's code is published. My first video, entitled "How to Make a Bow," has been watched more than 263,000 times and is a top marketing tool that encourages viewers to visit my site to purchase resource materials. Roger Green of Teed Up is hoping for similar results when his golfing videos are uploaded to his YouTube channel.

Establish your business's channel today by creating a YouTube account even if you're not yet ready to make and distribute videos.

Google+

If you were online when Google+ began, you read lots of comments about how it was created to compete with Facebook and how it would or would not succeed. The story that matters to us is that Google+ is another option to gain traction in your industry by creating circles of people who are similar professionals, customers, or even focus groups to spread your message through photographs and text. While this sounds similar to Facebook, you are free to experiment here and find out who to connect with on Google+ that isn't easily accessible on Facebook, Twitter, or LinkedIn.

As an example, a good friend of mine who's profession is mentoring women about social media landed a guest appearance in a Google+ chatroom with Gayle King (good friend of Oprah Winfrey) because my friend responded to a question asked by King in Google+. That appearance was recorded live and now broadcast worldwide, providing my friend with expanded media promotion she couldn't buy at any price.

How did my friend get this opportunity? She set up a Google+ account in her name and business name. Then she made a list of people to follow and added those people to her Google+ circles. As with Twitter, even if those people didn't follow her, she could still read their messages and respond. Now my friend is known by a world-wide audience, some of which has invited her to speak at business events and asked her to write articles for their popular online publications.

Visit the Google+ home page to learn more about the program and to watch a video that explains the service. Set up your account page according to the Google+ instructions and examples you find on how others in business create their page. Like LinkedIn, Google+ also lets you set up a separate page for your business. Invite friends and family members to join you on Google+ so you can become familiar with it. Separate each group into a private circle so you can share information with them much quicker than by sending e-mails or making telephone calls. From there, search for business people, competitors, and potential customers to follow.

Learn more about Google+: www.google.com/+/learnmore

Pinterest

If your business or expertise is best explained through photographs, Pinterest is the place for you. After opening an account that prominently includes your business name (similar to creating a business page in Facebook), you begin creating pinboards displaying pictures about your business's attributes.

If you're a publisher, display pictures of books you publish. Wedding photographers share pictures of clients' showers and weddings. Chefs feature their latest food creations. Your expertise unfolds in a beautiful photographic display for people who are interested in your topic, business, or expertise to re-pin (copy) on their pinboards. That allows your pictures to go viral through sharing it with others on Pinterest, which can lead to sharing on other social media.

Most business owners find a way to market with Pinterest. However, if your profession is service-based (welder, plumber, electrician, etc.), similar to Janet Ross's accounting service, it may be difficult to determine what types of profession-based photographs interest Pinterest users, so bypass this program in favor of other social media mentioned above. Roger Green sees Pinterest as a great tool to display golf clothing and accessories, while Janet is planning how to structure her LinkedIn account.

There are many online options to market your business. You don't have to post information to all of them, though with practice, it won't be difficult to do so. As suggested earlier, it is wise to create accounts in all programs. A calendar or Excel spreadsheet allows you to decide what topic to market each month. That topic is then segmented into what to write, ask, blog, tweet, video, and pin, all leading to a URL on your website or blog for followers to visit for more information, subscribe to a newsletter, attend a teleseminar (we'll discuss this in chapter 6), purchase a product, or take another action that keeps them interested in you and referring friends, family, and co-workers.

Visiting social media channels can become addictive. You may find yourself spending inordinate amounts of time reading about other people. Is social media your profession? If not, guard your time wisely. Morning can quickly change to afternoon without you accomplishing anything on your goals' list all because you were mesmerized reading about other people's antics. Set a specific time during the day to post your messages and read what other people share. Focus on your marketing timetable and let nothing extraneous stop you.

Find out more about Pinterest: http://pinterest.com/about

In Person: Preparing to Connect with Like-Minded People

More marketing connections and opportunities occur when you meet people face to face, and it all leads to new accounts and sales. That's why mixers and meetings during breakfast, lunch, and after-hour events are more popular than virtual events you read about or attend on the web. Since people do more business with people they like and trust, make it your mission to add relationship-building events into your monthly itinerary. This section shares numerous marketing steps to take and not take when in the company of others.

Creating a Buzz with Business Cards

Whether standing next to an unfamiliar person at a local event or traveling with strangers on an airplane 38,000 miles above the earth, you're in the right place for a business card exchange. Some of my best connections have occurred in obscure places (hotel fitness rooms, conference center hallways, elevators stuck between floors, for example), and without having business cards available during impromptu meetings, lots of revenue would have been lost.

Don't for a moment think that business cards are obsolete now that social media and other web connections take center stage. It's the business card that reminds old and new acquaintances where to find your online real estate. It also informs holders about your brick-and-mortar location, free offers, or toll-free number, all depending on what you decide to print.

The business card is your personal billboard, reminding contacts who you are, what you do, and how your products and services benefit them, their companies, and personal lives. Success in business depends on your ability to put business cards in the hands of everyone you meet, wherever the gathering occurs. You'll be shaking lots of hands to get your business name in places where buyers exist, including business meetings, sporting events, and recitals, all which amounts to handing out cards during conversations. It doesn't matter whether business cards are exchanged at the introduction or conclusion, just so long as you make sure to complete the discussion by distributing a permanent reminder.

Business card information: www.solomarketingbook.com/businesscards

---

Business cards wield lots of power. They are also incredibly inexpensive, especially when you consider the part that distribution plays to increase your marketability. Most cards include basic information to ensure that prospects and clients can contact you in a manner that matches their preference:

- Your name
- Title or occupation
- Business name and/or logo
- Business slogan
- Address (street or post office box)
- City, state, country, zip or postal code
- Telephone number
- Fax number (if relevant)
- Website address
- E-mail address

The above list seems too extensive to include on thick, coated pieces of paper approximately two-by-three-and-one-half inches in size, but it fits as shown in the examples on page 34. You can elect to put everything on your card and also include secondary information (listed on page 33) as needed.

> **Logo definition:** www.entrepreneur.com/encyclopedia/term/82398.html

It's surprising to find that some new business owners overlook the basics when creating their first card. I often receive business cards without area codes, cards without a person's name, and cards that exclude the city and state. These omissions occur because the cards' owners expect to distribute their message only in local settings. Why not include all the information, especially since there's no extra printing charge to do so?

Graphics are another issue. You want your business card to be memorable, but not because of something disjointed, such as a symbol on the card that doesn't match your business type. If you don't have a logo, or if there is no symbol for your industry, a card without graphics is acceptable.

Street Address or PO Box?

Blog articles and message-board discussions on the Internet weigh the pros and cons of using a street address versus a post office box number on a business card when your office is located at home. What truly matters is your image, expertise, and professionalism at meetings and social gatherings. As long as you present yourself properly, no one will care about or question your address.

Three business card no-no's are misspellings, crossed-out words, and penned-in words. Business cards are too important for your image to appear messy. Double-check each and every line of your card before placing an order. Use a magnifying glass, eyeglasses, or reading glasses to inspect every character, and also have a trusted person review your cards before printing. If your address or phone number changes, order new cards immediately. The price is quite affordable, and gaining new business through card distribution is worth the investment.

Here are secondary details to consider including on the front or back of your business cards, depending on each item's importance to connect with customers:

- Cell phone number
- Instant messaging (IM)/screen name
- Telephone numbers for additional locations
- Toll-free number
- Your photograph (a tactic used frequently by real estate agents)
- Shipping address (if not the same as the main address on the card)
- State- or country-issued business license number (Service professionals add this to establish credibility)
- URLs to Twitter, Facebook, LinkedIn, or Pinterest accounts
- Hours of operation
- Location directions

Two Cards Double the Odds for Success

Many solo and home-based business owners cater to more than one industry. If this is true in your business, having two cards rather than one is a smart investment. For example, you may work with retailers and wholesalers within the same industry. Distributing one business card to both groups may not allow you to convey the right message in each case. Carrying two distinct cards works to your advantage.

Sample Business Cards

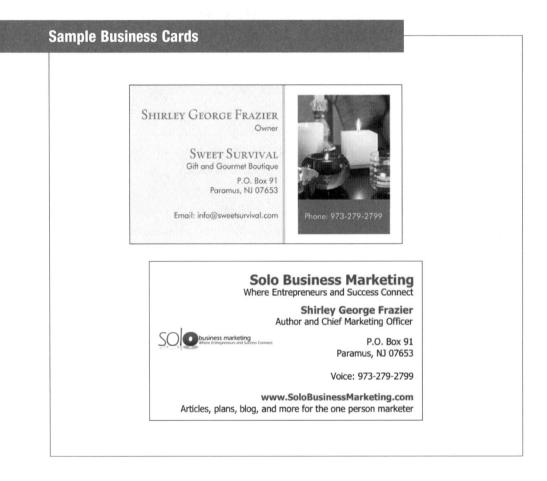

There's no need to change your business name when creating two cards, unless that's part of your strategy, but your slogan or phone number may vary. One group might receive a card with a plain, white background, while the other receives a card with color or in a fold-over configuration. This difference helps you easily distinguish between cards and thus present the correct one to a prospect.

To make matters more complex, there are more formats on the market than the traditional matte or glossy coating. Here's a short list of features business card suppliers offer.

Metallics. Silver, gold, or platinum is forged into a business card that's indestructible except when inserting into a shredder. This configuration may interest jewelry professionals or can signify a level of achievement in any industry. Keep this option in mind for upgrading purposes, not for creating your first card. Your money is better spent elsewhere.

Wood grain. Your name and all particulars are etched into a card that simulates wood. High-end construction companies may opt for this, and it's popular with companies that catch, sell, or distribute fish products.

Round edges. Business card makers are cutting corners, literally, smoothing 90-degree edges into round ends. The look is considered by some as a step up from traditional cards without being over the top. Women may prefer this style more than men.

Confections. Business cards made from chocolate pressed into molds have been around for years, created and distributed only when making an impression counts. The basic paper card is usually included along with the chocolate version in case the recipient eats the confection, leaving nothing but a sweet memory of your initial meeting.

You're charged with starting and completing so many marketing details that you can't possibly remember everything to include on your business cards. The Business Card Checklist on page 36 will help you pinpoint every detail to include on your cards before placing an order. When the cards arrive, remember to check them for accuracy and to distribute them briskly. It's time to tell everyone you meet who you are, what you do, and how your business benefits them.

Business Card Rules

Many new entrepreneurs distribute their business cards sparingly. This is unfortunate and counterproductive. Smart business owners distribute their cards as fast as humanly possible. To do this, you must carry your cards, without fail, wherever you travel while completing business and personal tasks. Try never to be in a position to say "I don't have a card" to a person who's ready to buy or recommend your service.

Business Card Checklist

Primary Details	Write Your Input Here	Check Here to Omit on Card
Your Name		❏
Your Title		❏
Business Name		❏
Business Slogan		❏
Business Address		❏
City, State	_____, _____	❏
Zip Code		❏
Telephone Number (include area code)	( )	❏
Fax Number (include area code)	( )	❏
Website Address	www. _____ . _____	❏
E-mail Address	_____@_____ . _____	❏
Optional Details		
Cell Phone Number	( )	❏
Toll-Free Number		❏
Additional Location(s) (Street/City/State/Zip)		❏
Shipping Address (Street/City/State/Zip)		❏
IM Screen Name		❏
Photograph		❏
Professional License Number		❏
Hours of Operation		❏
Location Directions		❏
Card-Buying Basics		❏

Commercial printers and business mail-order catalogs were once the only sources of buying business cards. Today the Internet dazzles us with new methods of putting the perfect message onto cards of any shape, quantity, and color. You may already have a stack of business cards on hand, but don't let familiarity with one printer stop you from discovering what's available through other sources.

As you evaluate potential suppliers, look for the one who meets your criteria. Your card's appearance is a major consideration, and so is price, which varies between local and online suppliers. You will want a company that creates cards to your specifications and have them ready for pickup or delivery in a timely manner. There's one more ingredient that completes this recipe: service. Service makes the difference between selecting one business card supplier over another. Once you find a supplier that meets these criteria, order your traveling billboards and be ready to distribute them wherever you travel.

Here's a look at the types of suppliers available to create your business cards.

Commercial Printers

These local superstars compete heavily against online competitors. Local suppliers make themselves known through neighborhood business groups, regional trade magazines, and charitable events. Their prices may not be as low as other suppliers, but the cost is still affordable. There are pluses: Working with local commercial printers keeps the region's economy thriving, and a relationship with this source can create numerous business opportunities that cannot be secured through online vendors.

Office Supply Stores

These retailers capitalize on location to offer more than the usual workplace products. While picking up toner, paper, and clips, you can browse through a large binder filled with business card styles and logos ready to order on the spot. Making a purchase is easy, and cards can be picked up usually within two weeks of the order date. As with any print order, you must make sure that no part of the card layout is overlooked. One disappointing experience may cause you to seek another supplier in the future.

Check out these supply stores: Staples www.staples.com; Office Depot www.officedepot.com; Office Max www.officemax.com

Web-Based Business Card Suppliers

Online templates make business card creation simple and easy. That's why Internet card suppliers enjoy growing popularity. Competition between card suppliers has dropped prices to new lows. But low cost does not always amount to a quality card, as some online purchasers assert from experience.

Ordering online means you must familiarize yourself with product terminology —"matte," "glossy," "100-pound paper," among other technical specifications. Business owners and others who've purchased business cards online give both glowing accounts and scathing reports about their experiences. Take these findings with a grain of salt as you perform your own research, which includes asking people within your industry and circle of friends which online suppliers deliver quality cards and great service.

> **Check out these online business card suppliers:** Moo www.moo.com; Vistaprint www.vistaprint.com

Software

Business card software, used in conjunction with your computer and printer, is another option that business owners choose for several reasons:

1. Cards ordered from an outside source won't arrive in time for an upcoming event, so temporary cards are created in-house.
2. Creative individuals thrive on the challenge of designing their own cards. When finished, a copy is delivered to an outside printer to reproduce it in exact specifications. Reproduction isn't always possible, but determined business owners find a way to make their design a reality.
3. Certain situations, such as the immediate need to promote a new product or service, call for impromptu cards. When there's no time to order through traditional channels, printing temporary cards on perforated business card paper, purchased at an office supply store, is a quick solution.

> **Business card templates:** Avery at http://bit.ly/ws9zz3

Business Card Follies from the Trenches

Exchanging business cards is an easy and forthright process. You hand one person your card as she reciprocates with her own. But you wouldn't believe how unnecessarily complicated business card distribution can get! Here are situations I've faced that show what not to do when exchanging cards.

The Cosmetic Kamikaze

Business travel can be exhausting, and it can also be exhilarating. There is satisfaction in spending time away from the office meeting people and sharing business tips. In addition, you travel back to the office to develop ideas collected at the event. During this moment of comfort while at the airport waiting to board a plane is when I'm most vulnerable, and that's when a woman approached me. She placed her business card on the chair's armrest and announced she'd soon return. I took one look at the card and saw her affiliation with a cosmetics firm. There was no doubt that a sales pitch was coming.

My premonition was right. She returned and began to unload information on all the benefits I would receive by selling cosmetics. Here's the problem: There was no formal introduction, no questions about why either of us is in town or about each other's expertise. She saw me as an opportunity rather than as a person with whom to build a business relationship.

This woman attempted to sabotage my peace, so I interrupted her and announced that I had no interest in selling the products she represents. She didn't listen and started her pitch a second time. That's when I said, "Have a good day," and began reading a book taken from my luggage.

Attempts to force-feed a new contact with your pitch is not the way to make a business card connection. However, it is good training in one aspect: This approach shows you how some people treat others under the guise of relationship building and warns you not to make the same mistake.

Not all people in the cosmetics industry practice bully tactics, but I've met my share. Some people want you to make a detour from your plans and join them. However, apples and oranges don't mix. If your business is operating vending machines, another person's encouragement to sell a product that takes you away from your core business delays your success. Wish the other person well, and stay on track. Continue searching for individuals who appreciate and respect the true reason for exchanging business cards.

The "Not Getting to Know You" Method

While waiting for a speaker to begin his seminar at a New York City conference, I sat in a room with other attendees and started conversations to discuss our backgrounds and uncover ideas on how we might do business together. It was a standing-room-only crowd, and everyone spoke in muffled tones as they waited for the seminar to start.

Another attendee walked to the front of the room and began distributing her business card to each of us. She wasn't the speaker; she simply started giving out her cards without saying a word. Some people refused to take the card. Others asked her why she was doing this, and she responded, "I'm just trying to network." Her plan was disastrous, and you can understand why. Business cards don't cost much, but they're not meant to be wasted. Not only was this an exercise in futility, but she also harmed her reputation and image.

Relationship building is about making connections, finding common ground, and sharing information that propels the success of both parties. Blind exercises such as this create no allies or business opportunities.

After hearing the speaker and making final connections, I walked out of the room and noticed the misguided networker's business cards left behind on seats and the floor. Hopefully she learned a lesson before her business dreams disintegrated.

Wasting Another Person's Time and Money

Trade shows are events where I conduct seminars. I also attend to connect with exhibitors, reinvigorating old relationships and learning about new products. But there was a time when I was on the other side of the exhibit table, marketing my products and trying new tactics to convince people to buy.

I must have participated in at least fifty trade shows, and at each one entrepreneurs posing as customers solicited me for business. Rather than invest in a booth to market their services, these impolite imposters attempted to take the time and money I invested in renting a booth to sell me on their goods. Anyone who has rented an exhibit space knows these tactics well. As a novice exhibitor I allowed this approach at my first event, but during the show some entrepreneurs were upset that I didn't spend as much time with them as I did with real customers. By show's end I had a box full of marketing materials from these entrepreneurs, which I left behind for garbage collection.

The next event was handled differently. When entrepreneurs approached my booth, I gave them my business card and instructed them to mail the package to me. Serious businesspeople who want to build their businesses will send the information to you by mail, along with a proper letter of introduction. They may also contact you by e-mail that includes a link to their website or blog. If not, nothing's lost on your end.

This type of situation illustrates why printing separate business cards is a wise investment. If you are a trade show exhibitor, distribute one card to legitimate prospects and hand the other card to everyone else.

Meeting Prospects and Clients Outside of the Office

Home is where we solo business owners make our money, working in a designated room with a computer, printer, and various technological tools. Home is also the place where babies cry, dogs bark, and dust bunnies gather when a broom isn't within reach, making it an inappropriate space to meet clients and allies. We need to get out into the world and make connections in open environments where others gather for the same purpose.

Army posters once featured a picture of Uncle Sam pointing outward and stating, "I Want You!" That's how hotels, coffeehouses, and restaurants feel about your presence in their facilities. They welcome your planned and impromptu meetings. They realize the profit potential from the small and solo business sector and, in the true spirit of marketing, will do anything to win your dollars.

Retailers and service organizations want us to come to them for informal meetings for several reasons:

1. They look busy. If lots of people are meeting informally, coming in and out at a steady pace, their location resembles a hub of excitement, the in place to be. Business owners prefer this type of setting, one with an energetic environment and tolerable noise level. Word spreads when a facility gains this reputation, and popularity is key to everyone's business success.
2. They sell products. Meetings tend to include sharing a meal or beverage. In the course of sixty minutes, one table has the potential to host three twenty-minute meetings. Such turnover keeps the register ringing all day long. This win-win situation allows the facility to maintain profitability while home-based owners make connections.

3. They become familiar, and so do you. Recognizable faces get perks, such as better seating and other incentives that infrequent visitors won't get. This benefits both parties. You can't predict how a first-time meeting will end, but your surroundings in this comfort zone will keep you focused and on track.

By catering to your need to meet outside of the home office, these facilities are happy to make cozy spaces available within their shops. They understand that the more comfortable you feel holding meetings at these well-lit and secure places—which in rural and suburban settings have plenty of parking as a bonus—the more likely you will be to plan larger gatherings at that location and order meals. More individuals are joining the business start-up bandwagon, which means more service-based companies will be searching for ways to cater to you.

Before you book a meeting, choose a day to visit the places in your area that are good sources for get-togethers. Weekend visits are no good. You want to experience each setting on a typical weekday, as your informal meeting will occur sometime between Monday and Friday.

Here are key features to check.

Configuration. Does the place have adequate seating during the day and time of your visit? Is a separate meeting room available in case you wish to speak privately with your guests?

Crowd. Are long lines of customers waiting for service because a skeleton crew is working at that time, or is the staff-to-customer ratio adequate to accommodate steady business as it arrives?

Cleanliness. How does the staff maintain the facility as customers move from the front door to the order counter to the seating area before exiting? Do napkins, stirrers, and spilled beverages litter the floor, waiting for a customer to be injured? How quickly do staff members address cleanliness, or do they walk with their heads tilted upward in an attempt to ignore hazards? Are tables dirty and sticky as though a group of third graders visited minutes before you entered?

Comfort. Does the facility seem to mind your visit if you work at a table without buying food or beverage? You'll know the answer if the staff watches your movement or informs you of a nonposted rule that says you must buy if you intend to stay.

Convenience. How far is the facility from your office? Is there lots of traffic in the area or noise inside the shop due to car horns or truck transportation? Reviewing each potential meeting place lets you know which one is easiest to reach, but a fast commute means little if the other attributes don't add up.

Your search may uncover other meeting nooks in your community, such as private library rooms and teahouses with designated meeting spaces. The teahouse expects you to order food and drinks, so choose a space that accommodates the meeting type.

The bottom line is this: Your business lifestyle makes you a hot commodity to facilities that recognize the profit potential of having you and others like you patronize their spaces. The number of home-based business owners is growing at a rapid pace. More meeting places are being planned right now by smart shops, restaurants, and others who recognize the value of accommodating entrepreneurs like you.

How to Fit Networking Events in Your Schedule

One thing that busy solo and home-based business owners have in common is time constraints. There are so many projects to manage and lots of opportunities waiting for attention that it may seem difficult to fit networking into your schedule. That's what I used to think. Because everything rides on your shoulders, making time to meet new people and greet old acquaintances can be limiting. Or is it?

Meeting people at events and using business cards to confirm connections are activities that guarantee a healthy, thriving enterprise. Sitting at a computer all day long does not. That said, the computer is a tool to make online connections as explained early in this chapter and continued in chapter 6. It's also a source to find networking events. Here are places to look:

- Business newspapers
- Technology websites that conduct nationwide seminars
- Business communities
- Local and national business groups

Business newspapers: Crain's www.crains.com
Technology websites: Microsoft www.microsoft.com; Adobe www.adobe.com;
Hewlett-Packard www.hp.com

Make a habit of reviewing your local newspapers. Business meeting news is usually printed on Monday, but your papers' schedule may differ. Most newspapers have an online component, so if you don't subscribe to the print version, check the newspapers' websites for a meeting calendar.

Networking meetings are different than conferences, which are all-day and multiday gatherings focused on a certain business or industry. The most popular meeting types are as follows.

Mixers

Expect a two- to three-hour event where people in business get together to relax and speak with as many individuals as possible within the event's time frame. Lots of people are meeting for the first time, and others are getting reacquainted with old friends and allies. Mixers have a tendency to be noisy events. Lots of people are talking at once, which makes for a decibel-elevating experience.

Business over Breakfast

These gatherings are attended by business owners who are too busy during the day for luncheons but need to get out of the office to refresh their focus. The breakfast menu varies, and the cost is nominal, especially in relation to the people you meet and the interaction that occurs in this sixty- to ninety-minute gathering. I favor this type of meeting because it gets you up and out in the morning when most business owners are fresh, idea inspired, and ready to interact with others in a casual setting.

Lunch and Learn

If you're searching for new people to meet and have two hours open in the early afternoon, then luncheons are for you. The gathering includes:

1. Interaction with peers
2. A sit-down meal
3. A featured speaker

The fast-paced atmosphere makes the most of your time and gets you back to the office for a productive afternoon. This is a terrific midday event for those who enjoy a break in their workday and cannot attend evening events because of family obligations.

Dinner and Dialogue

Dinner meetings feature a speaker who shares ideas to enhance your business. This gathering is more expensive than the other get-togethers mentioned here but not so much that it's unaffordable. Many business owners prefer to end their day by comparing notes with others and learning smarter ways to organize and streamline their workload. For home-based owners who cannot otherwise get out of the office, attending a dinner meeting can be a worthwhile investment.

You'll find other business gatherings in your area sponsored by the chamber of commerce, local clubs, industry-specific groups, and national associations. Groups that host these events understand that there is strength in numbers, so expect to be asked to join a group whenever you attend a function.

Avoiding Meeting Overload

Attending too many events in one week may cause you to become meeting weary. To make sure this doesn't occur, decide which events are better for your business at the present time. Every meeting will not be for you; choose the ones that match your current needs. Your selections may hinge on:

- Industries that bring together the most qualified leads
- Time of day that's best for you to attend
- Types of meeting you prefer (industry specific, meal and speaker, etc.)

Are you a person who doesn't like going to meetings because it's difficult to interact with others, yet you realize that such interaction is critical to your success? Then you're in luck. Every meeting is filled with outgoing individuals who are happy to introduce you to others. You'll feel more comfortable making your way through crowds of people with help from a group's ambassador rather than getting through it on your own. Call the event number and request such a person to guide you on arrival.

Be aware that shyness can work to your advantage, because your listening skills take control. Many people don't listen to others; they simply wait their turn to talk. You, however, will be ready to concentrate on each word spoken by the person in front of you, and that's the best way to learn and grow.

Seasoned business owners consider themselves pros when it comes to exchanging business cards and building relationships in person and online with customers and allies, but we all need a refresher course from time to time. That's what this chapter provides, a new and renewed approach to guarantee lifelong connections.

03

Put It in Print—Direct Mail Marketing Tactics

"Thank goodness for the Internet." That's the sentiment of home-based business owners worldwide who use technology to reach customers. No more counting solely on telephone calls and direct mail correspondence to individuals and businesses with words that convince them to buy. Yes, the Internet is excellent. The web put solo businesses on the map with twenty-four-hour-a-day storefronts. However, the web will never eclipse the need to market with direct mail, the process of connecting with clients through postal mail using letters, postcards, note cards, and other printed materials. Electronic and printed marketing work hand in hand to capture customer attention and make believers out of prospects who decide that what we have is what they want.

This chapter examines how to get attention through direct mail. Best of all, you'll realize that direct mail is affordable. You just have to learn where to find the goods and services that tell the world you're the best in the industry.

Why can't we use the web as our main marketing method and skip direct mail altogether? A report compiled in October 2010 by the US Department of Commerce, National Telecommunications and Information Administration, and issued in February 2011 entitled, "Digital Nation: Expanding Internet Usage," provides clear reasons why business owners cannot depend solely on the Internet to reach prospects.

- Percentage of US population with no Internet access from any location: 28.3
- Percentage of US households with no Internet access: 28.9
- Reasons given for non–Internet use:
    - Don't need/not interested—58.1 percent
    - Too expensive—18 percent
    - No or inadequate computer available—15.7 percent

These statistics lead to one conclusion: There are significant numbers of people offline. These people have no access to your website, so they call or write asking for information. My potential buyers often write or call me to ask for a catalog and other printed literature. I once told them to visit the website, but many said they did not have easy access. That let me know I was neglecting non-Internet buyers. This is why direct mail is and will always be an important part of the marketing puzzle, connecting us with people who want what we sell.

> **US Department of Commerce, National Telecommunications and Information Administration:** http://1.usa.gov/rncy5z

There's another reason why your marketing must include printed products. People with Internet access often want details by mail. They desire something in their hands that tells them more about your product or service.

To some, information sent by direct mail is seen as more credible than an item sold exclusively on the web. After all, anyone can create a website. There's so much on the Internet that's fraudulent compared to what's sold through printed mail, especially since business owners invest time and money to produce and send a letter, brochure, catalog, or flyer by mail. "Surely it's a worthy product if the business owner took the time to craft paper into a sales piece," some folks think.

Electronic or Print? Look to Your Market

Generation Xers (people born in the 1960s and 1970s) and Generation Yers (people born in the 1980s and 1990s) are big Internet users. They think differently from members of the baby boom generation, who did not grow up with computers in their homes and offices. Middle-aged and older adults respect printed materials. To them, a letter, brochure, or catalog gives an item more credibility. It's an art form that makes a product or service come alive with a mix of text and photographs. If you cater solely to customers age fourteen and under, perhaps the Internet is all you need. But if your target market is adults, creating direct mail products is a wise investment. The web cannot be your only marketing tool if you are to succeed in the long run.

This is what customers say to themselves. They want to hold a piece of paper in their hands, something that convinces them that your product saves time or lightens their load. When you visit a professional office—such as that of a doctor, dentist, or accountant—literature about their services is available in the waiting room. Brochures and newsletters act as informational pieces, and each includes a website address where more details are found. These professionals understand that a website is another tool that helps them win clients. This is the same way to view your site.

What if there were no Internet? You'd be forced to create direct marketing pieces, send news releases regularly to media personnel, attend trade shows where your products and services are shown, make television appearances, and solicit magazine quotes and advertisements all by mail. Even in the age of the Internet, none of these opportunities can be overlooked. All can be completed regularly as part of your marketing strategy, and all lead to sending direct mail to prospects that will migrate to your website for a closer look before buying, subscribing, or calling.

E-mail works as another tool in your marketing arsenal, providing customers with information about you in another format. Websites and e-mail both work effectively with direct mail, the more-expensive part of the trio due to the cost of printing and mailing literature to prospective customers.

Creating direct mail products was once incredibly expensive. In the past these products were available only through commercial printers, some of whom lacked the capacity to print graphics that add credibility to mailed literature. But thanks to modern technology, you can create direct mail pieces for a fraction of what it used to cost. You can work with a graphic designer who will ensure that your brochures include pictures as well as text, or you can select an online printer that will let you create your own products and ship them to your doorstep just in time to begin your marketing campaign.

E-mail as a Marketing Tool

Using e-mail as your exclusive client connection source, rather than combining it with direct mail, is quickly becoming a marketing obstacle. E-mail is a cost-effective way to reach customers because of the low-to-no cost factors, but people who regularly send unwanted or unsolicited e-mail have made e-mail a liability rather than a resource.

According to ClickZ Network, e-mail contact continues to drop in popularity because of spam-related mail and because filters installed by e-mail hosts (AOL.com, Gmail.com, Yahoo.com, etc.) decide which mail is to be delivered and which is flagged as spam. Unless a prospect is expecting your e-mail, your message may never be opened.

Still, e-mail has its good points. A person may request to see printed materials as a follow-up to electronic communication. Chapter 6 explains electronic newsletters and the role they play in aiding your sales effort. The same is true for offering direct mail information and catalogs to readers of your online newsletter. Anyone who requests a mailed offer trades his or her e-mail address in exchange for receiving printed material. This is a smart prospecting tool for any marketer looking to capture as much information about their newsletter readers as possible.

Words That Make Direct Mail Memorable

Emotion sells. It's that simple. Put yourself in the clients' shoes. Understand how they feel about a situation they're facing. What will you say to bring a sense of calm or satisfaction? What will relieve their fear or anxiety? These are the words that convince the prospect to buy.

You may be a pro at saying the right words but weak at putting those words on paper. If that's true, there are several places to find the words and phrases you need to craft your letters and other direct mail pieces:

Infomercials. There's no reason to reinvent the wheel when infomercials are filled with ideas and phrases to bring customers to your door. Record commercials that, in your opinion, do the best job at raising product awareness and closing the sale. Write down key sentences and add them to your brainstorming list.

Junk mail. Why wrack your brain to put words together when professional copy editors send you materials daily through postal mail? Most direct mail letters are two pages in length, and the envelope often includes a promotional message that you can rewrite for your own use. Review each piece of mail you receive. Extract and edit the sentences that get your attention and that you believe will keep prospects reading your materials.

Advertorials in magazines and on the Internet. Sales copy is everywhere, including in print at these two locations. Magazine ads state the word "advertorial" at the top of each ad page, and it's easy to find this type of sales material on the Internet. Just look for single page sites that seem to scroll down for miles. These pages are created to sell books, manuals, reports, training CDs, or teleseminars on a specific subject. Anything that mirrors the message you wish to convey can be considered grist for rewrites for your own sales copy.

The real work starts once you collect sentences and other ideas. You must change phrases so you don't plagiarize other people's work. Don't worry—there are enough words in your language to shape the sales copy. Changing verbs and sentences to conform to what you sell will become second nature over time. This rewriting is not difficult. Write your text using comfortable language, words that string together easily when talking face-to-face with a potential customer. Unless your prospect is in your business, try not to use jargon or industry words, or you may lose the chance to convert the person from prospect to client in the first paragraph.

Look at this example of how to change a sentence to suit your sales needs.

Sentences from mailed sales copy:

"You know opportunity when you see it. That's why you started doing business online."

Sentences after changes:

"You don't need another opportunity to do business online. You need a better one that gets you up and running in less time."

Your direct mail copy must reveal your product's benefits and strengths and, in some cases, a guarantee or money-back offer to seal the deal. Free offers and other incentives help change a "maybe" into "yes." Such offers include:

- Thirty-minute trial consultation
- Free evaluation
- Free shipping in one or both directions
- Complimentary account analysis
- Free report by mail or e-mail
- Free CD or DVD
- Free checkup of old or current system

Any of these items sweeten your offer. Only you know what converts a person sitting on the fence into a buyer. Note, however, that such incentives cannot be offered on a regular basis or they will lose their effectiveness. Many solo business owners introduce their firm by offering something new and different in addition to the main product. Perhaps a certain month is slow for business, and a free offer acts to generate interest. Some industries, due to customization or product limitations, cannot offer add-ons. Instead they opt to maintain a level of exceptional service. You will learn about options by reviewing industry magazines, websites maintained by leaders and competitors, and direct mail literature by networking with other industry participants.

Let's review the types of direct mail pieces that complement your website and review the reasons why each is relevant.

Letters

A letter is an assembly of words arranged in paragraphs that introduces your business to prospects in hopes of making a sale. Letters may not rate high on your list of direct mail tools. Perhaps that's because you've yet to receive a letter that made you take immediate action.

Letters produce sales. That's why millions of companies use this basic sales tool to connect with prospects worldwide. Letters are still considered one of the most inexpensive ways to sell. The part that takes the most time is crafting the content. Once the letter is written, you create a mailing list, run labels, insert the letter into the envelope, and mail. Creating the letter can be outsourced to a copywriter, but that's a pricey alternative. That's why using the language from other sales letters and recasting it into your own words is a smart strategy.

You can print, stuff, and mail the letters yourself, or these tasks can be outsourced to a virtual assistant or other trusted source. Some home-based business owners ask friends to help when mailings add up to a thousand pieces or more. When the work is done, the owner hosts a small party in appreciation, which can also turn into a network gathering or a brainstorming session focused around the completed work.

Determining which type of letter to send a customer is just as important as its content. Some letters are straightforward, providing information and benefits on one or several pages. Some add humor to make a point. Other letters work in conjunction with postcards, reply cards, and other devices to encourage the prospect to take the requested action. Yet other letters act as a test for similar types of correspondence to be used in the future. If letters you receive by mail don't convince you to buy, that's no reason to neglect letters as a tool to connect with customers. Simply gather the best ideas from those same letters and then rewrite them into ones that will ultimately bring you sales.

Different Letters for Different Clients

All customers won't receive the same letter. This is an important point. Tailor the introductions and endings to your prospects' characteristics. Large corporations segment their letters according to gender, geographic location, preferences, and other reasons. You may not be able to make hundreds of changes to one letter, but it is wise to make small changes, mailing two or three different formats according to your goal. (As you will see in chapter 4, this same segmenting applies to news releases, which are customized according to the media that receive them.)

Start by differentiating a letter's content and structure. In each case the first paragraph must instantly connect with a need or problem the reader is experiencing. That will keep him intrigued and wanting to learn more about solutions you offer.

On page 55 is a sample letter that Janet Ross, the CPA featured in chapter 1, uses to introduce her business to prospects. This letter was created using ideas and information found in several direct mail pieces, mostly service businesses selling insurance, software, and infomercial products. Accounting is serious business, so Janet must be straightforward to get attention.

The term "direct mail" details how the correspondence will arrive: by traditional means that includes an envelope (unless the correspondence is a postcard) and stamp to ensure delivery. But the word "direct" also focuses on getting the person's attention with words that uncover what she may be experiencing at the present time. Here's how Ross's letter gets its point across:

1. *Familiarity.* The first paragraph quotes a conversation that parallels a problem the reader understands. You hope to make a connection by having the reader say to herself, "Yes, I have that problem, too," and keep reading to learn how to solve it.

2. *Who you are.* Introduce your company as the firm willing and able to solve the problem. If you are in the same locale as the prospect, that can also be mentioned early in the correspondence, or you can add that fact in another part of the letter. A local solution, in some industries, is viewed by many as an asset.

3. *Experience.* Everyone wants a problem solver with a track record. Customize your letter with satisfaction gained from people in the same business structure (sole proprietorship, partnership, etc.) or industry.

4. *Flexibility.* Some prospects will have deep pockets and be able to pay any amount of money for what you offer. Others need sporadic help or a plan that fits their budget. Be sure to mention this in your pitch.

5. *Action.* Tell the reader what to do to initiate contact. Action ranges from making a phone call, sending an e-mail, visiting your website, coming into the office for a complimentary product or service, or mailing a postage-paid card. Direct mail readers need guidance; without it your mailing will be deposited into the trash.

6. *Finale.* A postscript, or PS, beneath your signature is said to be an effective reminder of an important point mentioned within the letter. That's why it's found in most, if not all, direct mail correspondence. A postscript can also be used to add a secondary offer.

All direct mail letters are created using one or more of these points, arranged in a manner that connects with readers. Janet's letter is one page in length. She knows that her prospects are time-stressed business owners, people who shy away from reading long-winded dissertations. A one-page letter identifies the problem and solution.

Other products or services may require up to four pages of explanation. For example, a newsletter publisher must document the reasons why an industry-specific newsletter costs $495 a year. The publication's features are identified using bulleted points, case studies, and endorsements from industry leaders. The hefty price tag calls for a healthy explanation of benefits.

Roger Green, chapter 1's golf equipment owner, could have taken the serious approach to reach potential customers. But because of the characteristics of his industry, he chooses to go the lighthearted route. The letter on page 55 shows what he plans to mail as an introduction.

Green's letter effectively grabs the reader's attention. However, there are marked differences from Janet Ross's letter due to the casual approach and competitive tone. The letter on page 56 shows how it connects with the prospect.

1. *Focus.* Feet, one body part that gets a workout on the golf course, is the addressee. Beauty salons may address a person's hair. A caterer's or tea shop's target is taste buds. Whatever body part is the main focus, within reason, is prime target for addressing within your letter.

2. *Strengths.* Others selling the same products and their weaknesses are mentioned and compared to your strengths. This is handled effectively without divulging competitive names. A laundry list of limitations is unnecessary; just one or two examples make the point.

3. *Convenience.* Bringing your wares to the reader, rather than having him come to you, is a premium in today's society. Mention any time-saving strategies and one-stop shopping advantages.

4. *Incentive.* Make sure that perks complement the package. In this example, socks and foot powder are gifts presented during the initial meeting because the reader's feet are the addressee. If using a straightforward letter, a package of tees or golf balls is just as valuable.

5. *Closing.* "Call us" is the preferred action. This lets the reader and you connect so that the best choice of products accompanies you to the home or office. Other options may not uncover as many facts as provided during a phone call.

6. *Enclosures.* A brochure is added in an attempt to gain the reader's confidence and trust. This reference tool serves to confirm details mentioned in the letter and leads him to a website for more information. The letter's last paragraph is appropriate, but it could have been used as a footnote or postscript.

An offbeat letter can win results, but stay within smart boundaries when ending the correspondence. Roger Green will sign his name in pen rather than add a footprint above his name.

Here are more ideas to begin and end your letters, taken from random direct mail correspondence.

BEGINNINGS

"You don't need another _____, you need a better one."

"As soon as you say so, I'll send you _____."

"Now you can get _____ for pennies a day."

CLOSINGS

"Your satisfaction is our top priority."

"If you're not pleased, we will refund your money and cancel all fees."

"This offer is available for a limited time, so act now."

Dear :

"It's hard to find an accountant who watches my finances and helps me keep as much money as possible," a woman told me today by phone, "especially since I can't keep up with all the financial options."

Do you have the same problem? AccountAble solves this and much more. I am dedicated to keeping your business in the black while you concentrate on the work you do best.

As an experienced CPA who specializes in small and one-person businesses, I make my company's services available on a monthly or hourly basis. You may need to contact me only two times a year to review your books and make recommendations. This is what many of my clients prefer and why I encourage you to consider this very flexible option.

My information kit will give you the full story. The kit can be accessed on the Internet at www.webpageurl.com. Or return the enclosed reply card, and I'll send you a free kit describing how I can work to keep more money in your pocket for reinvesting, retirement, and other needs.

Whether you're satisfied with your current accountant or are thinking of making a change, I urge you to visit www.webpageurl.com or respond with the enclosed reply card. There's no obligation, and your satisfaction is always guaranteed.

From experience, I've learned that the best time to evaluate an accountant is before you need one, not when tax time is just around the corner. Let me show you how AccountAble makes keeping your profits simple and easy.

Sincerely,

Janet Ross

CPA and Profitability Counselor

PS: Trying to decide which accounting software is best for you? Call me at (303) 555-2345 for a 15-minute, no-obligation discussion to learn your options.

Dear Mr. Hanson's Feet,

We don't often take the time to address other feet. But our concern is for your comfort, and that's what prompts us to contact you.

It seems that other golf retailers aren't giving you what you need: one place to find supplies, equipment, and individual training to keep your game at its best during match play and casual outings. But there's one retailer that is. Teed Up is the company to call rather than spend your time driving from retail shop to retail shop and speaking with salespeople who know little about you or golf.

At your convenience and at no obligation, we'll bring the golf course to you. You'll see a selection of golf products that fits your size and experience, all in the comfort of your home or office, and hear about our specialized instruction that keeps your game on par and on the green.

Other retailers seem to have cold feet about making your life easier by bringing golf product choices directly to you. Or maybe they're just dragging their feet. Who knows?

The next time you're ready to aim for a score of 60, remember that Teed Up is the *only* golf product and training facility that provides in-office service. We'll even bring you a pair of socks and foot powder so you'll be ready for long hours on the golf course.

Call us at (704) 555-6568 for a closer look at the products and services that will make you stretch, shake, and stay on par. Again, the appointment is complimentary—there is absolutely no obligation.

Also be sure to check out the enclosed "foot note" that explains our Tutorial-of-the-Month program and business buyers' incentives.

Sincerely,

Roger Green
Teed Up's Head Golfologist

Postcards

It is said that prospects take time to digest both sides of a postcard. That's because there's nothing to open, and its size accommodates a limited number of words, making it a means of disseminating information quickly and easily. Most business owners who mail postcards add a photograph or graphic image on one side, which grabs the attention of anyone who handles the item, including postal service employees. These are just a few reasons why postcards are adored by home-based and solo business owners. Here are three more reasons:

1. Cost factors make postcards affordable in any budget.
2. Creation takes less time than other types of correspondence.
3. Small amounts can be generated with your computer and printer, while larger quantities are outsourced to commercial printers or the many online postcard specialists worldwide.

There was no way I could work with a commercial printer in the early 1990s to create the type of postcards I wanted to distribute. Printers in my area didn't have the ability to produce a slick, glossy card. Everything was finished with a matte surface, which meant my message would arrive with an uninviting appearance. I would have wasted my time and money. My only outlet was to create postcards using my own computer and printer. Can you imagine using a Kaypro computer, dot matrix printer, and scored four-by-six-inch cards fed through the printer with a pin connection on either side? That's what I did. Whatever method that was available to make contact with the people most interested in what I sold was fair game.

Postcards either work in conjunction with other direct mail tools or they work alone to remind prospects and clients of your existence. For example, a marketer sends a letter of introduction along with an offer or incentive. Two weeks later a postcard is mailed to those same targets as a reminder of the letter. A second postcard, mailed two weeks after the first, ends this particular campaign by recommending a product or service and steering the reader to a website for more information. Aside from the cost for stationery products, $1.12 ($.46 + $.33 + $.33 = $1.12) was used for postage instead of the $1.38 it would have cost to mail three letters. That may not seem like a huge sum of money, but multiply the 26-cent savings by the number of postcards you currently send or will mail in the future. The reduced expense keeps money available for more products and campaigns.

Postcard suppliers on the web have gained popularity with home-based business owners and large corporations who need a simple product that draws lots of attention and ultimately many sales. Online suppliers have drawn criticism when the product isn't made to the buyers' specifications, but that's true of other postcard makers. Office supply retailers and local printers don't always get the order right, but their mishaps aren't as publicized on the Internet as businesses with web prominence.

If postcards are an option that fits into your marketing strategy, here are your design choices as well as their pros and cons.

Sample Postcards

Internet Suppliers

Web-based business card suppliers make postcards, too. Template choices are extensive, allowing you to select color or black-and-white images that draw attention when cards are retrieved from mailboxes. Postcard prices are affordable, and the price per postcard decreases as the order quantity increases.

There are dozens of postcard suppliers online. Review as many suppliers' sites as possible before committing the time to creating your perfect postcard. Read the FAQ sections to learn about the postcard quality (thickness, coatings, etc.) and types of available finishes (matte, glossy, etc.). From there, you'll be able to compare postcards on an apple-to-apple basis rather than just by price.

Pros. Abundant suppliers on the web. Quick turnaround from creation to delivery. Other marketing products available from the same source. Large selection of stock images. Easy-to-use templates on most sites. Some provide extra services, such as mailing your postcards when they're ready.

Cons. Templates difficult to customize on some sites. No-refund policies make rechecking work imperative. Post-checkout options increase the total cost if you're not careful. Some sites share your information with third parties (check each website's FAQ and terms of service).

Commercial Printers

Long gone are the days of massive two-color machines tended by printers who lacked flair and creativity. They've been replaced by graphic artists with Macintosh computers and the ability to take your artwork from conception to completion. These individuals, who are part artist, part printer, make themselves visible at local networking groups and business gatherings, often sponsoring an event in exchange for time to showcase what they do best.

Commercial printers are found in all regions, and it seems best to use one that's in your local area unless one outside of your region is highly recommended. Ask professionals within your circle for leads. When a person presents you with a remarkable promotional product, remember to ask who created it. You may discover a commercial source in your area that you don't know exists. Another option is to type the words "commercial printer" along with your state or city name in an Internet search engine.

Pros. In-house graphic artists create visually appealing, one-of-a-kind postcards. Local source builds another great relationship and your at-large network.

Cons. It may take lots of time to create and print your postcards. Start the creation process early. Price may be more than online sources.

Retail Office Suppliers

The same place that sells paper and pencils also supplies postcards ready to send by mail. Go to the store's copy center. You'll find a thick, spiral-bound book filled with pages of logos and colors that can be printed on business cards, postcards, and other quick-to-make promotional pieces. Your order is outsourced to another firm that subcontracts to the office supply store. You won't find any dazzling products here, but what the store offers may be suitable for you.

> **Retail suppliers:** Staples www.staples.com; OfficeMax www.officemax.com; Office Depot www.officedepot.com

As with every other type of postcard supplier, you must make sure that your preferred image and all of the information to be contained on the postcard is added to the order form. The store representative is assisting you, but don't place your faith in that person. These are your postcards, so review the order carefully before applying your signature and making payment.

Pros. Regional location makes access easy and convenient. Books are readily available at the copy or printing area to find what you want. Products are good for tradespeople, especially plumbers and electricians.

Cons. Very limited postcard choices. Vanilla appearance; nothing custom or outstanding.

Quick Postcards to the Rescue

I use the services of online postcard suppliers, but I also continue to create my own. Sometimes I need to print a quantity of twenty-four or forty-eight with a message that's limited to one mailing. When that's the focus, I turn to unprinted postcards sold in packs by office suppliers. They're available in small (four four-by-six-inch postcards per sheet) or large (two five-by-eight-inch postcards per sheet) formats, both in eight-and-one-half-by-eleven-inch sizes, the same as a regular sheet of paper so it feeds through your laser or inkjet printer. I use the smaller postcards. For me they're efficient, and the postage stays low while delivering my custom message. The larger postcards make a big impact as they travel from point A to point B, but the cost is the same as a business-size letter. Because of that, I'd rather use the small ones, but don't let me influence which postcard you select. Choose the product that's best for your marketing campaign. The larger postcards seem to be popular because they get noticed quickly in mailboxes. Perhaps they'll also work to enhance your promotions.

Newspaper Subscription Flyers

Did you know that local publishers will create a flyer, reproduce it, insert it into newspapers set for home delivery, and deliver it for you on a specified day, all for a nominal fee? If homeowners who subscribe to newspaper delivery are part of your target market, this is a great opportunity to connect with them. Think about it: You're a landscaper, plumber, or home cleaning specialist with plans to grow your customer base. You need a method to reach customers. Flyers placed within home-delivered newspapers may be your best route.

I learned about this process through a newspaper flyer added to my own home-delivered paper. It advertised the creation and distribution of 1,000 flyers for $700. Reaching 1,000 or more households at a rate of seventy cents per home is a bargain for some, especially those who offer a product or service for homeowners. One lead may net you ten times more than the promotion's cost.

This direct mail service is valuable because of other factors:

1. Flyers are sent only to subscribers and are not inserted in papers sold at newsstands. Sporadic newsstand buying would make your marketing campaign hit and miss, depending on who bought the paper on that day.
2. Promotions added to weekend editions, including your flyer, are more likely to be reviewed by subscribers in a leisurely manner. The newspaper's contents are scanned thoroughly on the weekend; during the week readers are more preoccupied and don't have time to consider your offer.
3. Publishers provide you with many distribution options, such as delivery to specific zip codes or homes rather than apartments.

A newspaper flyer is as basic as it sounds. It's one sheet of letter-size paper, printed on one side with details about your product, service, or promotion. It may include a photographic image that tells readers, in an instant, the type of product you are promoting. A border may appear about one inch from all sides. The flyer will not be a full-color product, especially for the price, but it may be printed on color paper. A newspaper account executive will send or show you samples of other flyers. Samples might also be available online.

Visit your local newspaper's website to find information about promotional flyers, or call the advertising department for details. Perhaps your local paper offers the service but only on a limited basis, or maybe it has never offered the service but will work with you to create a flyer that's inserted into home deliveries. Most large newspapers are owned by conglomerates that have a flyer distribution service. If you've never seen a flyer in your local paper, it means one of two things:

1. You don't receive the home delivery edition
2. No company in your area has tried this low-cost distribution service.

Although newspaper subscription flyers don't arrive in the prospect's mailbox, they are part of a direct delivery service that may stand out from letters. It's an alternative to consider if your service benefits the local community.

Sample Flyer

Clean Your Chimney Today!

Does your family breathe poisonous air all winter long because the chimney is clogged? What's up there that's harming your loved ones?

Clean Sweep Chimney Cleaners will remove debris, dead animals, and hazardous materials from your chimney. We'll install a new grate on top to keep cleanliness in and animals out. Don't wait any longer. Make an appointment today. Your family's good health depends on it.

Clean Sweep Chimney Cleaners
Call (904) 555-CLOG
Winter Special!
Call by September 15 and pay just $99.95.
Free gift with every cleaning.

Surveys

Business is going well. Clients seem to respond positively to the range of products and services offered by your firm. But is something missing? Is there an ancillary service that will clinch their loyalty? Does another company make ordering easier? A survey reveals the answers, providing solutions that self-brainstorming cannot uncover.

Sending a survey by mail gives you another reason to connect with customers, but this time they have a chance to tell you what they think. Everyone wants a say. Clients will be happy to provide input as long as you follow rules that they've set for satisfaction.

1. Determine the survey's focus so you get the most from the interaction. It's permissible to ask questions on a variety of areas. Perhaps you're about to launch a new product, or you plan to follow up on a service plan, or you need to know if a competitor's product is of interest to customers. All of these points can be addressed in your survey, but try to stay within limits.

2. Ask no more than twelve questions. Like you, clients have little time to respond. Choose the twelve most influential queries. If more than twelve are needed, stay within the limits of one sheet of paper.

3. Make the answer choices specific. "Yes" and "no" responses yield no ideas or solutions. Rather than ask, "Is the pie tart?" ask, "How would you describe the pie's flavor?" or "Describe the pie's flavor," followed by the answers: a) sweet, b) tart, c) bland, d) no flavor. This example has been simplified; answers in sentence structure are better for most surveys. In addition, include the word "other" and a blank line as an extra answer option for each question. This gives clients the opportunity to express themselves and to offer insights that you may not have anticipated.

4. Use the last questions to gather statistics about the respondents, such as gender, profession or industry affiliation, and geographic location. This will help you to find more clients with similar traits.

5. Give a deadline for submission. Most clients will submit surveys on time. A deadline will ensure that the largest quantity of submissions arrive by a specific date.

6. Offer an incentive, something that shows your gratitude for completing the survey on time. Incentives are anything from a discounted service to a gift card or other products. Most of all, the offer must be valuable to clients but affordable for you. Ask colleagues for incentive advice, and consult magazines that focus on the incentive industry to find a suitable trade-off that benefits both you and your client. (Turn to chapter 9 for an in-depth discussion about incentives.)

Incentive **magazine:** www.incentivemag.com

Premium Incentive Products **magazine:** www.pipmag.com

Before the advent of websites, surveys were strictly sent by direct mail. It's still advisable to send your questionnaire by traditional means. Mail your survey and include a postage-paid envelope. How often have you received a survey with no incentive notification or postage on the envelope? I can't tell you the number of times such mail has been sent to me, but I can confirm that none of them were completed. You need this information, so invest in round-trip delivery.

The survey's introduction is placed at the top of the page, before the survey questions begin. If you wish to notify clients that the survey is also available on your website, tell them in the introduction so they're aware of the delivery options. If clients are web savvy, they'll appreciate taking the survey online.

Surveys can be created as part of your website, or distribution is available through firms that let you create surveys online. Some online survey companies are free to use, but the free option comes with its own price: There are often limits on the number of questions as well as limits on responses. Other companies charge a fee for creation tools and enhanced services. These tools are viewed as gold by home-based business owners who need help with response numbers and other statistics available through paid sources.

Query your clients in eighteen-month to two-year intervals. Surveys distributed more frequently may cause SFS (survey fatigue syndrome). SFS is punishable by clients who vow to never again complete your questionnaires, open your mail, or visit your website. Surveys allow customers to provide you with ideas and insights that keep your company on the cutting edge. Ask clients occasional questions, but do not treat them like full-time employees.

Newsletters

Postcards give clients quick updates and announcements. Newsletters are structured to give a more in-depth look into how a business connects products and services with customers. They feature multiple articles on product uses, customer profiles, problems and solutions, trends, and more. Online newsletters, discussed in chapter 6, are delivered on a weekly, bimonthly, or monthly basis. The direct mail counterpart arrives monthly or quarterly. Why to consider publishing both a direct mail and an online newsletter:

Online version

1. Complements the website, leading readers to areas online related to articles or tips.
2. Helps to increase online shopping cart revenue.
3. Encourages readers to subscribe to the print version.
4. Increases blog postings and readership.

Direct mail version

1. Print component is read by clients who prefer text by mail.
2. Created using online version's ideas.
3. Clients often keep printed version as reference material.
4. Acts as an income producer if subscription fee is required.

I still have copies of my first newsletter, which was published in the mid-1990s. The eight-page publication was created by computer using newsletter software. I printed the sixteen pages on my printer and laid out the format for duplication at an office supply retailer, where public copying machines were available. The newsletter was published on eleven-by-seventeen-inch lavender-colored paper folded in half and saddle stitched to make the publication look neat and professional. Subscribers paid $12 a year to receive my news.

This print newsletter continued for several years before I decided to add an online component. Then I stopped the text newsletter because of the time needed to complete the project compared to the revenue it generated. Some industries thrive with both print and online newsletters, while other industries survive on just one version. Unless your newsletter is sponsored by industry corporations, direct mail newsletters require subscription fees to cover creation costs. This is a blanket statement; however, I don't know of any solo business owners who make a print publication available at no charge. It seems that the more your products or services cost, the more coveted the newsletter—and therefore you can charge a fee to create it. Lower-revenue industries cannot capture enough subscribers, so online versions are easier to create and stay in line with budgets.

If a printed newsletter holds the key to generating promotion and sales, there are ways to create that newsletter that keep you out of the office supply store waiting for your turn at the copier.

Industry Affiliations

In chapter 1, Janet Ross's marketing plan includes contacting two companies that create newsletters for accounting professionals. Such firms take care of the setup and distribution, placing Janet's name and her firm's information on the newsletter as if she were the person who created the publication. There may be a similar option for you. Industry publications, colleagues, and trade show exhibitors may be of service in locating an outsourcing service.

Online Sources

Type the words "newsletter creation" or "newsletter printing" in a search engine to find companies that provide this service. Companies still exist to create your customized newsletter because they recognize the need to reach customers who don't consider Internet-based products to be their sole or main news source.

Business owners in many industries successfully use print newsletters as a direct mail tool. The same may be in your future.

Note Cards

Note cards are a direct mail product that I highly recommend as part of your marketing plan. Sending cards to clients in appreciation of past business, for birthday or other greetings, or mailed in place of postcards and flyers will set you head and shoulders above competitors and others who sell just about anything. Note card greetings occur less frequently between client and service provider. It's becoming a lost art, but you can breathe new life into this simple technique that spreads positive word about your business around town and throughout the world.

My first note cards were made by the printer that created my stationery. A note card is included with every order mailed to clients. It expresses appreciation and good wishes for a successful business. If a client orders a second or third time, I search my customer database to make sure the message in the new card states something different from the first. It takes less than two minutes to write the note card, but I measure the connection in goodwill fostered rather than in time spent.

When I travel to speak at trade shows, many clients who have received my note cards thank me in person. Others say that the cards are posted in their offices as good luck symbols. I am honored and pleased to send this small token of appreciation. After all, the people who buy from me can always decide to work with someone else. Sending a note card with each order is the least I can do for clients ordering an average of $80 per sale.

Note cards are available through many sources. They can be made by the same printer that creates your stationery, ensuring that you have matching products to create a brand statement when contacting customers. Cards are available as a custom order through retail stationery firms. You can also buy different packs of note cards from retailers located worldwide.

Note cards need not be filled with world-renowned prose. Simply use words that remind, connect, inspire, or comfort. Two lines of text are appropriate, but sometimes you'll find yourself turning the note card to the back side to finish your thoughts.

How many note cards do you receive in a month? You can probably count the number on one hand and have five fingers left. Taking the time to write a note tells the receiver that you're the type of person who deserves to stay within reach. Aside from sending note cards to clients, I often use cards to connect with good friends, industry professionals, and other people I meet in my travels. I sent note cards to people I take to lunch, treat me to lunch, talk with me while flying, speak with me by phone, share a story after my speaking engagement, or act as my therapist when I complain about a business or personal problem.

Sample Note Card

TOP INSIDE OF NOTE CARD

June 28, 2013

Dear Sarah,

Just a quick note to thank you for considering our services. Busy professionals such as you need to stay focused on projects that increase revenue. I hope you'll consider us to concentrate on your profitability.

Wishing you success in business,

Janet Ross
AccountAble

There are people in your circle of friends, family members, and colleagues who do nice things for you as well as clients who deserve attention with a handwritten note. If you have no cards or cannot find a retailer with something special, look for a package at a supermarket or discount store. It doesn't matter where the cards are purchased. What matters is that the note card is prepared, signed, and mailed. That's the type of direct mail that separates you from all others.

Direct mail is a simple process that uses many forms of printed materials to introduce your business and stay connected with clients. Select the formats that realistically fit within your marketing strategy. Then use these tactics to dazzle everyone who connects with you, turning them into loyal and satisfied colleagues and clients.

04

Maximum Attention through Media Coverage

Getting press coverage in the local print or online newspaper must be easy. After all, both Hal's Hardware and Scrapbook City always get featured, so how hard can it be? Your business is much better than theirs. The local editor will spring into action after she receives a call or e-mail and hears why your product is the best invention since lined paper. She'll reserve tomorrow's front page to tell everyone what you sell, where you're located, and why your business is great. The phone will start ringing, sales leads will arrive by e-mail, and Internet orders will pour in. You'll become a millionaire all because of that one phone call or e-mail. It doesn't get any better than that.

Such dreams do come true, but not instantaneously. You're about to embark on a journey into media relations, the all-important world that connects your business with individuals and corporations that will soon become customers, hopefully on a long-term basis. The media work as a close ally, broadcasting your message in print, online, e-mail, audio, and video formats—as long as you follow certain rules. Finding the right media sources takes time and patience. This chapter shows you how to uncover news outlets and how to make the right impression with reporters and editors who will broadcast your news across town and around the world. Then chapter 5 will take your media relations one step further—onto traditional and satellite radio, TV, and cable.

You won't make a call or send an e-mail one day and be in print the next, but you will make inroads slowly and surely until print and online newspapers, as well as on-air reports, seem incomplete without your name, at least on a local level.

These are the main steps that produce media coverage:

- Create a list of story ideas to send to news sources.
- Write a news release tailored to the intended audience.
- Decide who receives your releases and how to contact them.
- Choose several news distribution options.
- Make a checklist to document distribution formats and results.

Now you're ready to learn about media coverage, where making news and securing relationships deliver the marketing success you envision.

An Introduction to News Releases

Rumors tend to be accurate, but the following one is off base, according to the editors who speak at media events. It says that the traditional news release is dead, that the media are no longer interested in this decades-old distribution format for educating, informing, and notifying readers about businesses locally and worldwide. There's no word on what is supposedly taking the news release's place, and that fact proves that the news release still reigns as the instrument to distribute business information in print, on television, and through web circulation.

> **News release definitions:**
> www.entrepreneur.com/encyclopedia/term/82372.html#;
> www.prnewswire.com/products-services/distribution/pr-toolkit/

A news release, also known as a press release, informs the media about a newsworthy event that promotes your business. A release is created for any number of reasons, from securing a new client to donating products to sponsoring an event. It can provide tips to educate potential buyers or shatter myths associated with your industry.

A basic news release may be structured in the following format. The first paragraph explains the main reason for the news. The second paragraph includes a quote from you or another credible source. The third paragraph provides statistics or expands on details mentioned in the first paragraph. The last paragraph states your company's credentials and contact information.

Not all news releases follow this pattern, but the outline gives you a good plan to follow as you begin creating and distributing newsworthy materials. On the next page is a press release submitted to the media during a crisis in the southwestern portion of the United States. It was published in local newspapers where the fires occurred.

Your news must contain details that inform an editor why it is relevant to the reader. The release's main focus is known as an "angle" or a "hook." It pinpoints why newspapers, magazines, and other media outlets need to share your news with the world. The angle in the above release piggybacked off a current news topic, which is why the media viewed the content as timely.

Each release contains one angle, and a news release on a specific topic can be restructured for numerous media sources that print news from different angles. That's how successful promoters get their releases mentioned in more than one newspaper or magazine. It may seem like a lot of work. However, if that's the way to get monthly exposure that attracts prospects and increases orders—all for the price of stamps or the time it takes to write and e-mail your news—it's worth it.

If your business sells to retailers, wholesalers, and consumers, those three angles are your focus in three separate news releases. The first paragraph is revised to make each group the focal point. An example of how to change a release to create a new angle is shown later in the chapter.

I learned to create a news release through books in local libraries. My library is still a favorite hangout. Although the Internet is widely used as a research tool, books are considered to be a more credible source for information. The books I consulted provided in-depth tutorials on what to do and not do when creating a news release. I started submitting my news to my local newspaper, and I wrote several releases that weren't published. Library books warned me to expect very little or no press coverage at the beginning. It's a rite of passage to expect, but don't let that deter you. An editor may file the news without your knowledge. Then one day a story develops, and the editor calls you as a local source to provide expert quotes.

The moment my news was featured in a newspaper column, I felt as if I had won a marathon. My news release writing style became better, and the media rewarded me with many quotes and feature stories. Once you learn how to match your news with a current event or industry trend, the same will happen to you.

FOR IMMEDIATE RELEASE

Contact: Shirley George Frazier, Day/Evening (555) 555-5555

NEW REASON TO DOCUMENT VALUABLES BEFORE TRAGEDY STRIKES

Paramus, New Jersey (July 3, 2013)—What happens if your home or apartment is lost to a fire or flood, and there is no record of your valuables? That's the question homeowners and renters who are victims of the fires raging in Arizona and Colorado face today.

"Homeowners' journals are selling fast," says Shirley George Frazier, president of Sweet Survival LLC, an international retail consulting firm. "Property owners across the country are realizing the importance of listing their valuables, documenting serial numbers, and photographing their possessions, and then placing all of the information in one concise book," explains Frazier. "The journal is updated each year and placed in a fireproof box at a secure facility outside of the home. That ensures that the journal's contents are preserved if tragedy strikes."

According to the National Fire Safety Board's 2011 report, more than 1.3 million fires were reported in the US causing $11.7 billion in property damage. More than 10 percent of homeowners' claims are denied because there is no proof of ownership included with filings. Creating and storing a journal listing valuables and home improvements can increase claim approvals.

In business since 1990, Sweet Survival LLC provides start-up and marketing assistance to entrepreneurs, retail store owners, and gift industry wholesalers. Shirley George Frazier is an author and professional speaker who has won numerous business awards, appeared on CNBC and The Food Network, and is frequently quoted in trade and consumer magazines. For more information, contact Frazier at (555) 555-5555.   ###

Why News Releases Are Vital to Business

Few activities provide as much media buzz as a news release, especially when it's tailored to match the media's specifications. It rates as high as networking or as creating a dynamic website or blog that captures corporate or consumer interest.

Developing and submitting one news release every month has the potential to bring business to you in ways never imagined. Once you start to see the possibilities, submitting news stories will become as habit forming as the work you jump out of bed to do each day.

That said, it's easy to sink into a rut or become disinterested in creating your monthly press release. Everyone operating a solo business experiences this type of temporary drought. However, when you win new accounts, sponsor a Little League team, or receive an award for businessperson of the year, that's the type of news that gets media attention. When you fail to write a release, you decrease the potential to attract new clients each month. You may not see it right away, but your profit-and-loss statement tells the story.

When I started my business, I was determined to get press coverage. One release, written about flavor trends in the gourmet industry, finally brought me prominence—a front-page story with a large, color photo under the headline. Orders and additional publicity poured in. That's what can happen when you're patient. Here's a short list of what occurred as a result:

- A newspaper publisher ordered twelve Christmas gifts from me for staff members.
- An insurance agent requested 150 gifts for her clients.
- A Food Network producer called to book me as a guest.
- Several trade publications requested expert quotes for upcoming articles.
- Subsequent articles were featured in trade publications and in a different section of the local newspaper that featured Mother's Day gift trends.

The above happened before the Internet became popular. This next list reveals new potential now that technology has expanded.

- Requests come from high-profile blogs asking me to write articles for their audiences.
- Invitations arrive inviting me to speak at colleges and conferences.
- Phone calls and e-mails from well-known publications ask for and print my opinion.

Once a newspaper prints a feature story or anything that includes you as a source, it's time to make the most of your limelight. First, check the publication's website to see if the story is available online. If so, place a link to the story in your website. Simply copy and paste the article's online address and add a caption that highlights the link to your website's home page or another notable page, such as in your online media room. (We'll talk about creating a media room in chapter 5.)

Many newspapers keep articles available online only for a short period of time, so check the link once a month to make sure it's still accessible. It's okay to quote your part of the article in print or on your website as long as you attribute the quote to its original publication. A better option to linking the article is to create a PDF (portable document format) of the entire article and place the copy within your site's media room so it's always available and accessible.

> **PDF definition:**
> www.merriam-webster.com/dictionary/pdf

Making duplicate print copies of news stories that feature your business is another smart idea. Include these copies with print materials you send to customers and media sources that request information by mail. That technique convinced the Food Network to schedule me as a guest.

Other ways to expand your fifteen minutes of fame include:

- Using the transcript to elevate you as an industry expert (see chapter 6).
- Offering to speak to groups for fifteen to twenty minutes on your expertise, exposing you to a wider audience of interested buyers.

How to Determine What's Newsworthy

The information printed in daily newspapers reveals what the media consider important to readers. Very few papers will mention a grand opening unless it's part of a column where such announcements are welcome. When sending information to the media, your mission is to educate, inform, and explain to readers why what you sell is beneficial to them, their home, business, family members, or whatever the end users seek to make their personal or professional lives easier or better.

The products and services we sell take on a human quality when we talk about them. That's because to us they are living, breathing extensions of ourselves. But the language we use to describe our wares and the information sent to the media must tell a different story. For example, you may believe that your service is the "greatest" or "easiest" on the market, but such words will not be printed by a credible journalist. I can guarantee that no one who interviews you in general media circles will add those flowery adjectives to a description. Remember that "newsworthiness" stresses timeliness and how your product or information benefits the public.

Here are ideas to create news that reporters prefer to print:

- How a product for newborns provides a restful sleep or teething relief.
- A sponsorship or donation to a local charity and why that group was chosen.
- A free in-store, office, or online contest, along with prize information and entrance details.
- An innovative way you're outsourcing business or hiring employees, and how it supports the community.
- A marketing option that's different from anything else being done in the area and the benefits that make it worthwhile.

The media also take interest in your news when a video and/or photographs on your site, blog, or Pinterest page accompany the story.

My first news release, written in 1990, was poorly crafted even though I spent lots of time in the library researching how to create an exciting story. I wrote and submitted news every month and sent it to local editors covering business, lifestyle, home, and health sections. Most business owners understand that change comes gradually, and when attempting to attract the media, patience tends to wear thin over time. I knew the tide would turn and that an editor would call me, so I continued to submit what I hoped were better-written news releases.

Here's what the library books taught me:

1. Use plain, white paper rather than stationery when mailing your release. Editors receive lots of releases on colored paper, but plain paper stands out.
2. The body of the release must be in either one-and-a-half- or double-spaced format, and each paragraph is indented.
3. Address your envelope to a specific editor. A generic title such as "The Editor" brands you as a person who is unwilling to research the correct person's name and therefore is not a candidate for news coverage.
4. Put the "who, what, why, where, when, and how" in the first paragraph, if possible. Editors scan mail quickly because, even in the Internet age, they receive hundreds of releases each day. The important points are to appear at the beginning to keep their interest. One exception to this rule is shown in the sample release on page 77 where the story starts with a human-interest focus. Nonetheless, the release still includes information about who, what, and where at the start.

5. Add the angle. Write the release in an informative style, not in an advertising format. If your news is about opening a store or having a sale, it's likely to be trashed unless a well-known entertainer or public figure will attend the launch.

6. Most editors prefer not to be called and asked, "Did you get my mail?" "Will you print the release?" "When will it appear?" Very few editors will answer these questions, and most are too busy to take such calls. You'll know if it's printed, because it's your job to monitor the media outlets that receive your news. In addition, the editor will generally contact you by mail or e-mail for more details if the story is chosen for publication.

7. Type "-30-" or "###" at the end of the release to indicate completion.

These rules still stand today when submitting your news by mail. However, many reporters prefer e-mail contact, which is explained later.

Press Release Dos and Don'ts

It's one thing to describe how to create a news release, but seeing the real thing provides a visual blueprint to get the media contacting you as soon as possible. You've seen one option at the beginning of the chapter. Here's another that shows how not to write a release (before), and the follow-up showing the edited version (after).

The "before" news release is similar to an advertisement, using clichés and jargon such as "cutting edge" and "business model," terms that customers won't necessarily understand. The "after" version introduces a human side to the story, which draws media attention and informs the public about the company's free skills-building workshops. The latter release also mentions that photographs are available. If you have photos of students training on-site that can be released for publication, let the media know by including this sentence directly under the contact name and phone number.

In short, look at the way good news articles are structured. You'll no doubt see that none of the stories are written in terms stating, "We're the best, the fastest, the greatest." Many stories spotlight a particular company, but other topics focus on stories that inform the reader of his or her rights and options as well as provide ideas for business or personal use. Think about this as you develop a press release. Anything submitted to an editor that's self-serving will be tossed into the garbage. Rather than writing that a product or service is "the best thing since sliced bread," explain the benefits to society, the business world, or everyday people.

NEW COMPUTER TRAINING COMPANY TO OPEN

Technology Tigers is the name of a new, cutting-edge training facility that's opening on Friday, January 4. It will offer classes in word processing, spreadsheets, and how to surf the Internet.

Company president Roy Robins and trainer Sandy Smith will teach most of the classes. The company is searching for more teachers to grow the business model.

As more and more people look to learn new skills, Technology Tigers will be there to help.

The address for Technology Tigers is 125 Any Road in Buffalo. To sign up for a class, call the company at (555) 555-5554.   ###

Technology Tigers
125 Any Road
Buffalo, NY 10836
Phone: (555) 555-5554

FOR IMMEDIATE RELEASE

Contact: Roy Robins, Day/Evening (555) 555-5554
Photographs available on request

Buffalo, NY (January 4, 2013)—Laid off from her factory job of 20 years, Beverly Taylor was scared and had to make a decision: Should she file for unemployment and hope to make ends meet, or would learning new technology skills allow her to make a rewarding career change?

Taylor, a Buffalo resident, enrolled in a free trial course at Technology Tigers. The 12-week class taught her how to create documents using word processing and data management software. Taylor now works as a freelance consultant for two firms that hired her to manage work flow.

Technology Tigers is once again offering free, trial courses throughout January as part of its New Year, New You month. Roy Robins, president, started the Buffalo-based company in January 2010 to help retrain individuals downsized from long-term jobs. "Residents need to be retrained after working for one company for so long," said Robins, who has worked in technology for 30 years. "Once our clients learn through the free trial, they come back for other training to keep their skills up to date." Technology Tigers also specializes in training staff on-site at employers' facilities.

For more information about free courses and upcoming classes, contact Robins at (555) 555-5554, or visit the Technology Tigers' website at www.BuffaloTechToGo.com.

###

Getting the Media Involved

Many businesses add another aspect to a press release that editors and reporters value: participation. Invite a reporter to be a trainee at your facility or a chocolatier for the day at your store. Suggest that the reporter bring a camera crew to film the process on-site. That's the type of priceless publicity available when a reporter is invited to get involved. If participation is being solicited, it's wise to e-mail the reporter about the special event to ensure that the person is able to attend, placing it on his calendar as soon as possible. Two week's notice is adequate. A telephone call to confirm the reporter's attendance is also acceptable.

Think about how your product or service helps the community, provides health relief benefits, gives moms a rest from the burdens of new motherhood, relaxes overworked individuals, brings joy and comfort to seniors or hospitalized patients, or educates the public about personal security. These are the angles the media yearns to print. You started a business because of a need expressed by individuals or corporations. Think about marketing with that specific angle in mind. From there you'll be able to create a news release that has the potential for local and international distribution.

What if Technology Tigers hasn't yet opened its doors and doesn't have a satisfied customer to quote? A free training day can still be promoted to show potential clients what they can expect when signing up for the service, and reporters can still participate in the opening day festivities. That's the hook that gets attention. For this scenario, here are the first two press release paragraphs.

Free training courses in word processing and data management will be offered throughout January at Technology Tigers as part of its New Year, New You celebration. Roy Robins, president of the Buffalo-based firm, opened the facility in January 2010 to help individuals who are unemployed.

"People need to be retrained after working for one company for decades," said Robins, who's worked in technology for 30 years. "Once our clients learn new skills through the free trial, they come back for other training to keep their skills up to date." The company also specializes in training staff on-site at most employers' facilities.

A certified public accountant (CPA) is another type of solo business owner who may be unaware of ways to create newsworthy publicity. Janet Green might start by writing articles to educate readers within her specialty. If focusing on personal taxes, articles submitted to the media explaining how to choose accounting software provide a welcome story. When working with corporations she might turn to industry trade magazines to submit a column or story that explains new tax laws that trigger audits, which educates corporate readers and pinpoints Janet's expertise. Other angles are available to write similar articles for different types of accounting clients. In addition, the media will publish information about free seminars to be held at libraries and other public facilities. Attorneys, veterinarians, insurance agents, and many other solo and home-based business owners benefit from this same newsworthy focus.

Every business has an angle that gets news coverage. Think about the main focus of your firm and promote that angle to its fullest potential.

Deciding Who Receives Your News

Just because you are a participant in one industry does not mean that other industries and groups are barred from receiving your press release. Many industries work together and count on each other for longevity. That makes it your duty to know about and participate in the industries and groups that depend on your information to keep them up to date on the latest trends according to your research.

For example, a caterer sends information about her business to trade magazines, but depending on her specialty, the caterer has many options for distributing additional news. Consider these ideas:

- Lifestyle or food sections in the newspaper get menu-planning tips.
- Senior magazines receive ideas on keeping salt or sugar content low while maintaining taste.
- Weight-loss newsletters, blogs, and magazines get substitution tips to keep foods low in fat and calories while high in flavor.
- Baby magazines and websites receive tips to make natural foods rich in nutrients to aid babies' development.
- Party planner publications receive a list of trendsetting foods that parties are ordering for guests.

Pick and choose the ideas for promotion in the circles that gain you the most publicity. A caterer may not use every option, but this type of brainstorming uncovers multiple methods to keep the caterer successfully marketing through sharing expert ideas and tips.

If your target market reads different publications, it's wise to consider all the options to keep your name in the spotlight. Customizing story ideas means you will be contacting various editors, and that's what we'll address next.

Finding Editors to Receive News

Editors are individuals who receive our news releases. They read a submission and make decisions to report it immediately, file it for future reference, or discard it. Some business owners wrongly believe that once a story is submitted, the press is obligated to print it. They're not. Consider the *New York Times*'s slogan: "All the news that's fit to print." The word "fit" refers to the newsworthy aspect of your story, not space constraints. I've met many *New York Times* editors and have submitted news to them. To date nothing's been published, but that doesn't mean I won't continue to submit news for future publication. You may experience more immediate results with smaller, local newspapers. That's what worked for me.

No product or service can be sold without researching the marketplace, and the same is true for finding editors and journalists to whom you submit news releases. Understanding the topics within each reporter's scope (also referred to as what they "cover") and how they craft news stories is critical to getting your information printed. You may not have time to read every article an editor publishes. That's why it's suggested that you skim articles to get a sense for how the editor selects news-worthy material. This research saves you lots of advertising money because you need not pay for ads when press release submissions gain you more promotion and sales than buying expensive advertisements.

Regional US business newspapers: *Crain's* www.crains.com
National US newspapers: *Chicago Tribune* www.chicagotribune.com;
Los Angeles Times www.latimes.com; *New York Times* www.nytimes.com;
Wall Street Journal www.wsj.com; *Washington Post* www.washingtonpost.com;
USA Today www.usatoday.com
Business magazines: *Inc.* www.inc.com; Bloomberg *Businessweek* www
.businessweek.com; *Entrepreneur* www.entrepreneur.com

Place the following media sources, as each fits into your marketing plan, at the top of your print or online reading list:

- Local newspapers (news that affects your immediate area)
- Regional newspapers (news from other counties and surrounding towns)
- Regional business newspapers (distributed at meetings, found at selective newsstands and vending machines, and sent by mail)
- National newspapers *(Chicago Tribune, Los Angeles Times, New York Times, USA Today, Wall Street Journal, Washington Post)*
- Industry trade magazines (non-newsstand publications mailed by subscription only; also found at trade shows)
- Business magazines
- General consumer magazines

Not all publications will be part of your research list. For example, local and national newspapers might bring you better coverage than a regional newspaper. Consumers may not be your focus, so that media market is omitted. You understand the target market. Searching through new media sources will prove beneficial to reach more of the target or another market segment.

Part of your research includes learning about the types of newspapers and magazines your clients read. This will help you connect with them more often as well as with others who have the potential to work with you or contract your services.

You can research and select newspapers and editors on the weekend. Go out on a Saturday or Sunday and buy all of the newspapers and magazines that could potentially receive your press releases. Then find a room in your home or office and get comfortable. Set up your laptop or tablet, or use pen and paper and take plenty of notes, including:

- Newspaper names, addresses, and websites
- Editors/Reporters and their sections
- Editors'/Reporters' e-mail addresses and Twitter names (Each section contains a reference box stating the preferred way to contact editors and reporters.)
- Types of section features (how-to, columns, questions and answers, etc.)

You could always visit a library and capture the same information there, but you may find it wise to buy some publications rather than review borrowed copies.

Use the "News Release Distribution" chart at the end of this chapter as a guideline. The Research Date column next to the editor's name lets you record when you last checked the editor's name and title. Editors and reporters are employees. They rarely keep their jobs for life. Wherever you submit news, you must check the editor in each section every few months, updating your checklist to reflect changes. It's a mistake not to confirm that the contact person is the same each time news is sent. Quick verification keeps the lines of communication open and strengthens ties with the media.

Fifteen Proven Tips for Great Media Relations

Getting mentioned in the news will always be an important marketing function for us solo and home-based business owners. Results take planning and patience, and that's why you are not to give up if one, two, or ten of your releases aren't published. Remember that you are not alone. Professional press release writers get the same nonpublished "results" as you. But many don't accept the results gracefully. During a New York press relations breakfast meeting, I was astonished to hear how editors are treated by professional press relations firms that don't get the coverage they expect. Some of the PR folks are rude by phone and leave messages in foul language for editors who do not promote an event or product launch. You cannot expect to get mentioned if you make enemies of the very people who are in line to become allies.

The editors who spoke at the breakfast work in business, consumer, and television media. They reiterated that tried-and-true marketing techniques were still the norm, and they shared tips that consistently get attention no matter where you live and work. As you move forward to find editors for getting your name in the news and building on your success, keep these fifteen techniques in mind:

1. *Focus on big issues.* Certain topics get lots of press coverage. This includes health, major holidays, the Internet, and baby boomers. Tell editors how your product or service benefits any of these markets or others that are hot topics in your area. This increases the chance for media coverage.

2. *Use e-mail to make contact.* Media contact by e-mail is better than snail mail, telephone, and fax. Make the subject line short and to the point. Create a release that's brief and focused, following the outline for a mailed release. Don't deliver news that mirrors a commercial! Be clear about the benefit to the reader, putting that news in the first paragraph.

3. *Double-check e-mails for misspellings.* Review your message thoroughly before clicking the Send button. Incorrect spellings, sending your message to the wrong editor, and forgetting to add your telephone number, e-mail address, and/or website link won't put you on good terms with each media contact.

4. *Build relationships.* Get to know each editor's section. Consider contacting the bureau chief, another editorial person who approves stories featured in each publication. Their names can usually be found on newspaper websites.

5. *Become familiar with their world.* The more you know about the media and how it operates, the better your chances for coverage in print, on traditional and/or satellite radio, on television, and on the Internet. This is a must to get your marketing message accepted faster.

6. *Try not to use a cell phone to leave a message.* But if you do, make sure to speak clearly and state your phone number twice in case the message is garbled or difficult to understand. The reporter will not track you down to return the call.

7. *Put patience at the top of your list.* Don't get upset if the media don't respond to your first, second, or even third news release. There are many reasons for silence, including holding the idea until it becomes a hot topic or waiting for a reporter to return from an assignment.

8. *Plan ahead.* Newspapers and television shows may contact you quickly for an interview or feature story, but magazines work with a five- to six-month lead time. If you sell heating supplies, plan to contact a magazine editor with tips or a story idea by May or June, months before the cold-weather season arrives. Keep this in mind as you schedule your releases, especially if there's a seasonal aspect to your business.

9. *Be above reproach.* Stretching the truth, telling fibs, and similar tactics are sure to be discovered (especially because of online technology), so it's best to promise only what you can deliver. One violation will make a reporter turn his back on you for good.

10. *Write envelopes by hand.* When sending information by mail, hand write the envelope. It's a personal touch and almost guarantees that the envelope will be opened more quickly than typewritten or computer-generated mail.

11. *Consider column submissions.* Newspapers and magazines feature columns that may be perfect for your story. Be sure to review column topics in case your business can be profiled in this section.

12. *Include statistics when possible.* Numbers always get media attention. Mention pertinent data within your release, and verify the source in relation to the story idea.

13. *Avoid double pitching.* Offer your news story to one reporter at a time within the same media source. Reporters don't appreciate learning that you've been featured in different parts of a newspaper or magazine within the same issue.

14. *Prepare for evergreen topics.* Certain stories are covered every year, such as how to save money heating or cooling a home, keeping weight under control during the holidays, and gift ideas for Valentine's Day. Be ready to pitch along these lines if your company fits the category.

15. *Start a blog, and update it often.* Blogs are now more popular as a source for expert information, and your blog's topic may get you as much or more coverage as news releases.

Blogs are often compared to journals. When you visit a blog, the date that each entry (also known as a post) was written appears next to, above, or below the post. For home-based business owners, blogs are more than journal entries. They provide you with an opportunity to promote your expertise through written communication often complemented by videos and audios. There's no limit to the number of postings shared with readers, and you can post to your blog often or randomly. Creating a blog is a smart move for today's business owner. See a sample blog at www.SoloMarketingBook.com. Chapter 7 will help you get started if you don't already maintain a blog.

Follow these tips carefully. Violate them and you're sure to sabotage your media coverage. Remember, you have a vested interest in making sure your story gets printed in as many media outlets as possible. Ensure that the relationships you start are built on a strong foundation so that you can approach each media source repeatedly.

Using Editorial Calendars

Every magazine and some newspapers create an editorial calendar, a yearly schedule of approved topics to feature each month. Many of these calendars are posted on media websites; if so, such information can be beneficial in your planning. Using these calendars dovetails with tips 8 and 14 mentioned above.

For example, if a magazine will feature a report on greeting cards, and you own a greeting card company, you will want inclusion in that feature story. Therefore, you must contact the editor about a month before the editorial deadline shown on the publication's calendar to be considered as an information source within the story.

I monitor multiple editorial calendars during the year, contacting managing editors when I see a story that will garner publicity. The tactic works most times. The letter on the next page is an example of what I send by e-mail when contacting an editor to propose my participation.

Connecting with Print Media

Adding tips within the initial introduction tells reporters that you are an expert with ideas to share and someone who will make their job easier. If you are contacted for story inclusion, be ready for an editor who's on a tight schedule. You'll receive a set of questions to be answered by phone or e-mail, whichever is best for both of you. Let the editor know when to expect your answers, and stick to your promise. The earlier you respond, the more the editor will appreciate and remember you. Once you've sent your answers, keep the questions and responses in a folder within your computer. You'll find the data to be helpful the next time an editor requests your participation.

When the article is published, request additional copies of the publication. If the article is available online, be sure to attach a link to your website, or because links tend to break without notification, create a PDF of the online article and post it on your website or blog.

Remember to send the editor a personally written note after the article appears in print. The words "thank you" are inappropriate in the journalism world because they suggest favoritism. Do not send a gift, as that is considered a bribe. With that said, you can still express your appreciation. Following is a sample note I've written on a personalized business note card.

How to Get Media Attention

Dear ___,

I'm Shirley George Frazier, an international gift and gourmet consultant in business for 23 years and owner of Sweet Survival LLC, a specialty marketing firm located in New Jersey. Please consider me as a contact for your upcoming report on cakes, pies, and cookies scheduled for the November issue. My clients, some of whom sell confections, receive three tips from me on maximizing their sales.

Piggyback on manufacturers' ad campaigns. This relationship strengthens whole-sale ties while helping customers find a local source.

Participate in industry calendars. Costs are split between 12 or more companies, and the calendar is distributed to thousands of buyers.

Place your money on cause marketing. Donate a portion of sales to a charity that will promote your business in their campaign literature.

Additional information can be found on my website at www.SoloMarketingBook.com, or you can reach me by return e-mail or telephone at (555) 555-5555. Thank you for your consideration.

Shirley George Frazier

Media Appreciation Note Sent by Mail

Dear ___,

Tea retailers are certain to find great ideas through your recent article, and I'm pleased to have shared my insights with your readers. The article will help tea sellers increase sales by choosing the best flavors for their customers.

Contact me if I can be of assistance in the future. I'm always happy to provide tips for industry participants.

Yours truly,
Shirley George Frazier

Online News Release Distribution

Editors are one group that will read your press releases. Then there's another group that wants to *distribute* your news. The Internet is where you'll find many free and paid venues for online promotion at the touch of a button. The number of online distribution services seems to grow every day, but the real question is whether or not to include them in your plan. Will these services net you better, adequate, or insignificant results compared to contacting editors directly?

An online news release distribution service is a web-based outlet that assists large and small businesses, in all industries, gain media attention to promote new products, services, and newsworthy events on a no-fee basis or for a nominal cost. These services accept press releases from businesses with a legitimate marketing agenda. In other words, websites selling pornographic products and illegal services are not accepted for press distribution. Those services don't seem to need promotion. It's the rest of us who require help.

Free Distribution Options

When I first became aware of web-based press release services that spread news to media outlets around the world at no cost to me, I had only one question: What's in it for them? One answer is that these distribution services encourage you to pay for additional press distribution over and above that provided through the free option. But the reason is not important. The services exist for your use, free or otherwise.

You can find numerous distribution services through Internet search engines. You'll be required to subscribe to each service, creating a user name and password to access your account. Create a bookmark in your Internet Favorites folder called "press releases" or another memorable name. This bookmark, which is accessible through your Internet browser (Internet Explorer, Firefox, etc.), saves the website's address so that at the click of a mouse, you easily return to each press release submission page.

Each distributor requires specific information when submitting your news release. This information helps distribute your news to the right media sources in the most expeditious way. You'll be asked for:

A submission date. Distribution services provide you with guidelines as to what submission date is permissible. A date two days ahead of time is normal. For example, if today is June 1, a generally accepted submission date is June 3 or later.

An article summary. What's the basis for your news? The summary is often captured in the first paragraph. It's okay to use the first two sentences of a release as a summary as long as it capsulizes the release.

A distribution category and subcategory. This is a breakdown of the industry to which you belong and any subtopic for the featured release. For example, if you own a pet products company, the category may be "retail" or "pets" or "animals," with a subcategory of "accessories." Subcategories aren't always required. Look at the long list of categories before making your choice.

Main keywords. Create a list of words from the release that best describe its content. This will help reporters who are looking for certain topics find them through keyword selection.

After creating your account subscriptions, follow this blueprint to submit your news:

1. Write your news release. Use the information explained in this chapter to develop one release for distribution.
2. Sign in to each web account, and complete the submission form. Double-check your work to make sure each area is complete.
3. Once the release is submitted, you will receive a document number from most distribution outlets. This number will let you monitor the release's processing and final publication.
4. Add each news release link to your own website for easy access by anyone looking for the latest information about your business or industry. Your online media room is the best place to feature the news release link. (See chapter 5 for more on media rooms.)

Service Upgrades

You'll notice that distribution services offer added options at a cost. While free options bring you limited publicity, paying for expanded distribution can put your news into the hands of reporters who regularly depend on releases featured on Yahoo.com, CNNMoney.com, Google.com, and other well-known sources.

It's unclear why most, if not all, free releases aren't featured through the popular news sites. However, part of your plan may include investing less than $100 to upgrade a release you wish to distribute in wider circles. Depending on the industry, topic, and keywords used, you may find that paying for upgraded service gets your news featured on the popular Internet news sites as well as in print publications.

Conduct research to determine if the service upgrade is worthwhile. This includes visiting online message boards and blogs to ask participants about their experience.

Review each distribution service's investment costs and the news outlets that are promised to receive your release. Create a checklist to document your findings, and choose the site that gives you the best distribution for the money.

Results will vary whether you select the free or paid option. Solo owners have found success in both cases. Timeliness and your chosen industry affect media coverage, which is why the outcome differs from person to person. If you have a terrific message to broadcast and can afford the low investment, move forward without hesitation.

Paid Distribution Options

Some services operate on a fee-only distribution basis. That's because they are at the top of the distribution chain. These outlets are the best sources on and off the web for press release delivery not only because they've existed for years, before the web became the great tool it is, but also because they work hand in hand with the media sources we know well. This includes the *New York Times,* CNN, and regional newspapers that provide wide coverage in areas that are otherwise difficult to reach.

In many cases paid services are news bureaus that send your release directly to the editor in charge of the section that covers your particular industry. If you believe that sending your news through this source is a wise decision, in place of or in addition to direct contact with reporters by mail or e-mail, then this strategy is one to try.

When you visit the paid news distribution sites, you'll notice that they guarantee distribution in the regions you specify. Your news release will be delivered, but just like news sent through the less-expensive option, it may or may not be published, so results also vary here even though you pay. The wider the distribution, the more you pay, and the costs are expensive for most solo and home-based business owners. Still, the chance of seeing your name in the news is more likely with the paid distribution services than with the free ones. This is one area where "you get what you pay for" still applies.

Paid Distribution Channels:

PRNewswire www.prnewswire.com; Market Wire www.marketwire.com

---

The options for media coverage can overwhelm a busy business owner. The urge to take advantage of each option is powerful, but putting every task on your list is not a smart decision, especially at the beginning. Brainstorm the possibilities, select the best course of action, and publish your news releases each month to increase media exposure and the publicity you deserve throughout the year.

News Release Distribution Worksheet

MEDIA SOURCE	MEDIA NAME Address/Website	SECTION/FEATURES (how-to, Q&A, etc.)	EDITOR Name/E-mail Date of Research
Newspapers			
Local			
Regional			
National			
International			
Magazines			
State			
Industry (trade)			
Specialty (food, etc.)			
Trade			
Newspapers			
Magazines			
Web Distribution			
Free			
Paid			

05

Making Yourself a Broadcast Media Darling

If you're eager to get up close and personal with potential buyers by way of radio, television, and cable, this is the chapter to learn all about acquiring your fifteen minutes of fame. In media terms that's five three-minute segments, each of which seems like a lifetime during a live broadcast! The payback can be enormous, and so can the preparation if you sell a product that's demonstrated on the air or offer a service in a tight niche. But where else can you find an audience of that magnitude, no matter what the medium?

> **Niche marketing definition:** www.entrepreneur.com/ encyclopedia/term/82588.html

Why Broadcast Media Want You

The concept of a show—whether on television, cable, or traditional or satellite radio—is to provide programming of interest to the target audience. Each show is manned by at least one producer, and her responsibility is to find guests who bring ideas and insights to viewers or listeners. That means every year thousands of people will be invited to share their message. One of those thousands will be you.

Why do the media search for people to fill broadcasts? Airtime costs money, and the media seek advertising dollars from companies with deep pockets to pay for broadcasts. While your focus is to deliver a dynamic presentation, your segment is generating thousands of dollars for the station.

Which media markets are best? Many broadcasts are available to host your appearance, but only the shows that match your unique message are the best to make your short list of candidates. There are other considerations to ensure that you select the right media sources to promote what you sell:

- Is a visual or spoken message best? Products are better demonstrated on television and cable, while someone offering a service can use either traditional or satellite radio or TV as a sales tool.
- What does the target audience prefer? If buyers listen to traditional or satellite radio during the morning commute, it may be wise to approach those shows.
- Is it better to focus on local or national promotion? Knowing where the most likely buyers are located helps you to decide if local stations are the first priority or if going after media with national distribution is the best approach.

Should You Seek Help to Get Broadcasting Publicity?

Outsourcing the job of finding publicity is worth consideration. Professional media relations specialists, known as publicists, work with and have access to show producers and other important contacts in broadcasting. Publicists exist to help clients find media segments, taking the work out of your hands so you can concentrate on other projects. A publicist provides a smooth transition to get your face and/or voice into millions of households, cars, homes, and offices around the world. But this help comes at a price—from several hundred to several thousand dollars. If you want to work with a publicist, you'll have to decide if the cost makes sense when compared with the expected results. Review the publicist's track record and get that record verified by a handful of the publicist's past clients. Ask for details of real benefits received through the alliance.

Like anything else in business, a publicist cannot guarantee results. She looks at what you have to offer, decides which avenues to take to proceed with media contact, and moves forward to pitch your expertise by e-mail, regular mail, telephone, or social media. Many solo and home-based entrepreneurs act as their own publicist because their budgets temporarily don't allow them to hire one, a role I accepted and explained in the introduction. Publicity is another part of the marketing puzzle that's achievable if you're ready for broadcast fame.

A Do-It-Yourself Primer

Your Public Best: The Complete Guide to Making Successful Public Appearances in the Meeting Room, on the Platform, and on TV, by Lillian Brown, was my bible for finding and preparing for my first television appearances. At the time the book was five years old, yet even by today's standards the book's content is relevant and contains these smart facts:

- Contact the show's producer, not the on-air personality.
- Find producers' names in media books found in the library's reference section (today you can research producers' names on media websites).
- Wear a color other than white, especially on the upper torso, when appearing on television.
- Sell the producer on the informational benefits or expertise you'll share with the audience rather than the actual product or service.
- Ask if makeup will be applied at the television or cable studio. If not, be ready to take the shine off your own nose.
- If makeup will be provided at the studio, look up when eyeliner is being applied. Otherwise close your eyes when your face is "under construction."

Now let's incorporate those tips into a broadcast-savvy publicity plan that will push your marketing campaign light years ahead and result in many sales.

1. *Make a list of all media outlets available to you.* That includes television, cable, and satellite and traditional radio stations. This is done by researching broadcasters in your area that welcome guest appearances. Look for show producers' names on media websites. Names won't appear on the home page, so be ready to drill down through levels of pages to find the right contacts. Sure, this is a lot of work, but it's worth your time if you want to appear or be heard on a particular show.

   Keep in mind that there are many more stations available that are not in your area. Regional shows are good starters, but consider the bigger picture. Look for shows with mass appeal that reach smaller, targeted markets.

   Consult the *Gale Directory of Publications and Broadcast Media* in your local library or online. This massive reference book lists media sources you may not have considered, complete with contact names, titles, telephone numbers, and e-mail addresses. Document your findings on your computer or tablet, or make copies of the Potential Media Sources Worksheet and fill it in as you go.

With list of markets in hand, decide which broadcast type is the preferred outlet for your product or service. This decision depends in part on whether your product needs to be seen or if traditional or satellite radio will work to spread your message.

2. *Create a press or media room on your website* to provide general information about your business and specific insights on your expertise. Many websites contain media rooms, so don't reinvent the wheel in deciding what type of information to include in your own media room. If you type the words "press room" or "media room" into a search engine, you'll find thousands of pages belonging to businesses in all industries. Ideally look for media rooms that belong to competitors and related professions. This will give you a good start as you put your page together. Over time you can add more material to your press room.

3. *Create a compelling statement explaining the product's or service's benefit to viewers and/or listeners.* Match your marketing to seasons, upcoming events, and current trends to make your appearance a timely benefit. Write this marketing script, also known as a pitch, on paper so you know exactly what to say when the producer picks up the phone. Writing your script ahead of time ensures that you don't fumble over words. Practice your pitch several times before calling to make sure your voice is smooth and confident. (Read the case study sidebar for an idea of what to include in a successful pitch.)

4. *Send follow-up information in whatever format the contact requests.* Such materials include a letter of introduction, product sheets, interview clippings, and letters from satisfied clients. Be ready to send these marketing materials by e-mail or express mail. In most cases you won't have to send information by mail, since many producers prefer the immediacy of e-mail over mail or fax. Ask each contact if e-mail attachments are acceptable or if another format is preferred. Then send the details as quickly as possible.

Getting your first big break on television or radio is a thrill. Soon after that you begin looking at your publicity efforts very critically, focusing your energy on marketing to audiences who are ready to buy from you. Everyone wants to appear on national television and cable shows, as well as traditional and satellite radio stations with hundreds of affiliates or large audiences, but will you get as many sales from them as you do from local markets? That's what you test and research, and then you make your decision based on what's best in terms of time and monetary potential.

Potential Media Sources Worksheet

Media Type/Show Name	Location (Address, Phone, Web)	Audience (Local, etc.)	Producer's Name/Phone/E-mail	Date of Contact/ Comments
TELEVISION				
CABLE				
TRADITIONAL RADIO				
SATELLITE RADIO				

In the mid-1990s I designed gift baskets, a product best shared with audiences through television. I studied different shows, watching each segment to determine where I fit in. I consulted library books, as the Internet was not in existence, to learn about target markets and to find other shows that would benefit my business.

The first show on my list, hosted by Robin Leach, aired at 10:00 p.m. on the Food Network. White-collar workers ages twenty-five to forty-nine and living in the New York City metropolitan area were the target. I believed these viewers wanted to see my product. My mission was to speak with the producer and convince him to let me appear.

I had learned that if you cannot find the producer's name ahead of time, the best course of action is to call the studio and ask to speak with the show producer. That's what I did. Armed with a script that explained the benefits viewers would receive from my appearance, I called the Food Network and asked to speak with the show's producer. The phone rang, and a gentleman answered.

"Dwayne King."

"Hello, I'm Shirley Frazier. I'm a big fan of [show name], and I'm also a gift consultant. Summer will . . . "

"Hi, Shirley!"

Without thinking, I pulled the phone from my ear and glanced at it. I thought, *I'm calling New York City. Who gives you a warm and cozy feeling during the first conversation?* I quickly pressed the receiver back to my ear.

"Hi, Dwayne! Summer will arrive next week, and I'd love to show your audience how to create picnics for two in the comfort of their home. If you're interested I'll send you some photos and other details to see if it's right for the show."

"That sounds great. Send it to me, and I'll take a look."

I quickly wrote Dwayne's full name and address on paper and started thinking about what to send him. A glossy black folder with inside pockets on either side looked attractive. I began gathering materials to fill the folder: my letter of introduction, business card, newspaper press clippings, picnic basket photographs, a list of individual and corporate client names, and copies of appreciation letters.

I attached a label with my business name and telephone number to the front of the folder. The package was complete, but it seemed lifeless. Something was missing, something that would dazzle Dwayne and influence him to put me on the show. I thought about Robin Leach and what to include in the package specifically for him. Because Robin is originally from the United Kingdom, tea and cake came to mind. I searched my gift basket inventory and found an English teacup and saucer and Earl Grey tea. I packaged freshly baked shortbread cookies and then wrapped the cookies, tea, cup, and saucer together with cellophane and topped the gift with a bow. The gift and folder were placed in a glossy black bag with cord handles. Everything was ready for presentation.

The package was too important to entrust to postal handlers, so I decided to deliver it by hand. I called my mother and asked her to accompany me to New York City. We were on our way in less than an hour.

The two of us and the package sailed through the Lincoln Tunnel (one of the main arteries between New York and New Jersey) in record time. Two trucks were parked in front of the Food Network building with enough space between them to tuck my Dodge Caravan. The delivery plan was working.

My mom remained in the car, poised to drive around the block if she was told to move the vehicle.

I entered the building, excited and breathless. One of the security officers gave me an entrance pass and I was on my way to the thirty-first floor.

Dwayne wasn't expecting me, so I left the package with a Food Network receptionist. I left the building moments later. The forty-mile round-trip excursion and delivery took just forty-five minutes.

An hour later I received a call from Dwayne. He loved the package and promised to try and book me on the show. Dwayne and I traded phone calls all summer. I never appeared on the show, but Dwayne shared my folder with another producer with whom I secured a relationship. My persistence paid off with numerous guest appearances on another Food Network show, which produced lots of publicity and many sales.

Satellite Radio

Your opportunities to be featured on radio have expanded thanks to satellite programming. Local stations are your first priority. Beyond that, your radio marketing research will include Sirius, the leading satellite station that hosts numerous talk show formats. Once you review their lineup, there's high probability that you'll find one or more shows to contact for an appearance.

Sirius: www.siriusxm.com

Just as you watch television and cable shows to locate broadcast markets, so must you listen to satellite radio. Subscribing to satellite radio at a cost of $14.50 to $18 per month, not including the receiver price and other accessories, may be more than your budget can handle. In that case, look for free trial offers. The free option may not give you access to every channel, but you can view the lineup on Sirius's website. See which segments fit your marketing plan. When you achieve success contacting television show producers, you can re-purpose the same approach with satellite radio stations.

Tell everyone about your desire to be a guest on television, cable, radio, and satellite programs. Spreading the word has the potential to uncover sources and insiders whom you didn't know, and great discoveries usually occur in your own backyard. For example, a neighbor's brother may be affiliated with a radio station, or a church deacon might work for a major cable network. It's smart to use word of mouth to broaden the marketing potential.

If you do not know of or cannot find anyone to help, do what you do best—use your ingenuity. That includes areas covered in this chapter:

- E-mailing or calling show or segment producers.
- Using library books and the Internet to uncover broadcast stations.
- Delivering a marketing package to a show producer.
- Creating an online media room.
- Downloading a free trial of satellite radio and listening to broadcasts that match your marketing needs.

A Word about Gifts

In today's post–September 11 security-conscious world, I suggest that only informational documents be given to producers rather than gifts of any kind. Buying products becomes costly, and it doesn't guarantee an appearance. In fact, gift giving at the beginning of a business relationship or after the segment concludes may be inappropriate. It can appear to some as preferential treatment toward the person who presents the biggest or most-expensive gift. Many broadcasters frown on gifts, no matter what you've heard or read in the press.

Broadcasts—Live or Taped?

Preparing for media marketing opportunities consists of being ready for every type of broadcast. It's almost guaranteed that a radio station segment will be live, but television and cable can be live or taped transmissions, depending on the show's format. Morning television shows are usually live, but shows aired on stations such as HGTV, Lifetime, and OWN are usually taped.

The live television format is quick, with no retakes or rehearsals. You are asked to arrive at the studio at a specific time, usually one to two hours in advance, to ensure you are on the premises and ready for the appearance. You and other guests gather in the "green room," a comfortable space that accommodates visitors before and after broadcast appearances. At a major network or its affiliate, this room will have chairs, tables, beverages, and snacks. Most guests do not eat before airing to ensure that their breath stays fresh. You are encouraged to also refrain from eating.

When it's time for your appearance, an escort takes you into the studio. A technician attaches a microphone to your lapel or collar. The show's host greets you and quickly interacts with you about the segment. You'll hear a countdown, which alerts everyone in the studio to the number of minutes or seconds before the broadcast is live. When the countdown reduces to 3, 2, 1—smile—and get ready to tell the world about your product or service. Everyone wants to hear why you're appearing on the show and how it benefits them.

One part of the producer's media package that wasn't mentioned earlier is the ten-question script that guides the host during the segment. You prepare these ten questions, which are designed to share with the audience a mix of basic knowledge about your specialty and some little-known facts. But be warned. Few, if any, of the questions will be part of the broadcast. Hosts seldom ask embarrassing or prying questions (though it can happen), but they might ask about a part of the business you haven't experienced.

Think about your responses before answering to lessen the *ums, aahs,* and *you knows* that are heard when guests fumble to find the right words. Such phrases are usually a sign of nervousness, which is common during the first few appearances. Don't fret if this happens to you. As with every experience, you'll learn what to do and how to combat the anxiety. Take a few breaths and, most of all, stay level-headed. The more you envision the broadcast as a casual conversation between you and the host, the more relaxed you become, and the best ideas and information will flow naturally.

This television and cable scenario also applies to radio, the only major difference being that your voice is the selling tool on the airwaves. Instead of recording directly from the station, you may be asked to call in. The producer will ask you for contact information to share with the audience. This will be your toll-free or general telephone number, website address, or other details that relate to the reason you're on the air.

Live television segments last between three to six minutes, while radio time depends on the show's format. When your segment concludes, you either return to the green room to satisfy your sudden hunger or leave the studio.

A taped television format takes longer to complete than a live segment, but the benefit is that the segment will play several times during a season, and it may be rebroadcast at other times in the year. Each person who appears on a taped show is given a certain time slot for taping. They are groomed, the area within the studio is prepared for their segment, and then taping begins. It can take several hours to finalize one person's segment. That means if you are one of three people to be taped that day, there's a chance that you'll be in the studio all day, especially if you're last on the list. Take advantage of the time by watching what goes on in front and in back of the camera. Talk with studio personnel, if possible, about other opportunities to appear on shows at that facility and similar places. Distribute and collect studio personnel business cards, and stay in contact with these folks. The connections you make here can go a long way toward landing future appearances on shows worldwide.

One person in particular with great insights is the makeup artist. She is privy to lots of information that you won't learn from studio executives, such as what perks to request when you'll be in the studio all day. These perks include travel expense coverage and a free stay at a nearby hotel the night before or after taping.

While you are in the studio, it is acceptable to ask the producer for a segment tape. If taping is live, you'll receive the DVD before you leave or later by mail. If your segment is taped and edited before being shown on television, it can take several months to receive a DVD. You want this recording to critique your appearance and responses, as well as to feature on your website or share with other parties who may consider you for upcoming shows and nonbroadcast speaking engagements.

After-Show Follow-up

Put your follow-up plan in motion before you leave the studio. Here's what to do:

1. Ask the producer for his card. Make sure his e-mail address is included, and ask if it's appropriate to make contact by e-mail or if another method is preferred.
2. Ask the producer when you can contact him again for another appearance. The timing will depend on what you sell, seasonal trends, and current events.
3. Contact the producer about two weeks after the show's airing. Give him figures on the responses you receive. This includes the number of people who visit your website and contact you by telephone, e-mail, and regular mail. Include the number of sales transacted due to your appearance. This information establishes your popularity and supports the reason to book a return visit.
4. Follow up to secure another appearance, as dictated by the time schedule set in step 2 above.
5. Ask the producer for the names of other show producers within that network if another show seems to be a good match to market your product or service.
6. Contact the producer when there's something of interest to ask or share. Do not e-mail him excessively or you will be labeled a pest and will not get another opportunity to appear on that network.

There is another follow-up component for you to monitor, and that is *results*. Now that you've presented yourself on air, think about the work it took to get you on television or radio as well as the time invested to make this dream come true. Was it everything you hoped it would be? Did you receive inquiries from viewers? And the final question: Is preparing for and appearing on television or radio worth the time and effort?

Inquiries, opportunities, and sales are what some home-based business owners experience each time they appear on a broadcast. For them such segments are
gravy. But for others—specifically those who must transport lots of products in their
vehicle, into a studio, and then back to the office—the process is either worth the
effort or a waste of time. Weigh your options each time you consider an appearance. Broadcast segments are golden opportunities. You may be asked to be part of
a broadcast every four to six months, depending on the topic and industry, but you
must consider the bigger picture. As long as you are reaping benefits, television and
radio are worth your time. If not, other marketing tools are at your disposal.

Do not expect overnight riches from your appearance. It will not happen. However, there is potential for rewards in the long run. Television and radio shows receive
millions of dollars in revenue from the advertisers who sponsor the shows. In turn,
the broadcasters have a responsibility to find suitable guests who will feed the viewers' minds and keep advertisers happy. You also have a responsibility, which is to find
the best broadcast to market your product and service to increase your store traffic,
website visitors, and revenue. Focus on your marketing plan to turn each appearance
into an advantage.

Independent business owners understand the difference between creating a new wheel and reinventing the current model. Most often we look for methods to mold the standard wheel into a version that works best to sell our products and services.

One way we can create a marketing path is to look at the campaigns of large and small companies. We decide what part of those campaigns are good strategies to target our customers. Then we search for tools within our budget to launch the promotions. Finally we create the product, distribute it in several formats, and track results. If the campaign was successful, we repeat the process when the time is right.

No matter what your profession, there are certain products that will always be affordable for you to create and clients to buy. These products are helpful on their own, or they are packaged as part of your service. Chapter 1 unveiled techniques to craft your marketing plan. This chapter shows how to develop ancillary products that complement the plan.

Here's an example. In the 1990s I recorded a fifty-five-minute cassette tape telling aspiring entrepreneurs about the pros and cons of starting a business. The tape sold for $15. I added a $10 coupon with each sale to encourage buyers to order other products. I believed the tape would be beneficial to introduce people to my business and provide a comfort zone that encouraged them to buy more from me.

The tape's format changed in the mid-2000s from cassette to CD when that format became more popular, and a DVD version was created as a visual alternative. I also lowered the cost by $5 to attract more buyers. The product continues to sell well because listeners can hear the message in CD format while walking, driving, or exercising and watch the DVD version at their leisure.

A friend of mine calls the CD version "mobile motivation," a phrase I added to my marketing message.

Whether you're just starting your business or are a seasoned professional, there are informational products and programs you can create to enhance your marketing plan. These include:

- Teleseminars
- Directories
- Web videos
- Online radio shows
- E-books
- Membership sites

Let's review these items so you determine which fit within a campaign.

Teleseminars

Consider this: You meet another expert in your industry whose name is instantly recognizable, or perhaps this person's insights are so profound that you're compelled to stay in touch with him. You ask him to be a guest on an interview you will conduct by telephone.

Your mission is to elevate both your name recognition and his through this teleseminar, which can be heard live by telephone participants and heard later by individuals who purchase the recorded conversation. Those who hear the discussion live are asked to pay a small fee, and individuals who visit your website can purchase the recording as an instant download.

Teleseminars are phone-based informational conversations featuring one expert, or it's between two or more people that educate listeners about a particular subject. Why consider adding this product to your marketing? It's easy to create, affordable, a way to educate people interested in a topic or profession, a method to elevate your expertise or industry status, and a revenue generator when marketed on and off the web as part of your existing products and services.

Speaking as a solo professional to a captive audience and acting as an interviewer of two or more people are two examples of how to host a teleseminar. Here are two more:

- You become the interviewee, which turns the spotlight on your expertise. This may be a better option than the two mentioned above, but there's a catch. You must find a person who's adept at interviewing, which entails keeping the conversation interesting and on topic.

■ You form a partnership with another person, and both of you present your information or views. This collaborative model keeps the content lively no matter which topic or industry is discussed.

Teleseminars are also part "mobile motivation" because they're easy to listen to while traveling when downloaded onto a mobile device.

I've teamed up with friends and colleagues to create teleseminars that discuss sales, marketing, organizing, and small-business law. The information is evergreen and sold in CD format at seminars I conduct worldwide. The CDs were once duplicated on my computer and labeled by means of custom software purchased at an office supply retailer before mailing them to buyers. Today, the preferred method of distribution is through a computer download available through an online shopping cart once the teleseminar is purchased through that same cart. If a buyer wants a CD by mail, that process is outsourced to a company that duplicates and mails the CD. A popular price for these CDs is between $29 and $39, but the price is adjusted higher or lower depending on the industry, subject matter, and any discount applied for multiple copies or orders placed during an event.

Value of Webinars

Webinars are another type of presentation that's considered an offshoot of teleseminars. While teleseminars feature an audio-only format, a webinar is an online free or paid event with information delivered in a slideshow (visual) format with the host or hosts narrating the slideshow materials. Webinars are marketed, scripted, and sold in the same manner as teleseminars.

There are three methods to market and sell teleseminars:

1. Charge a fee to listeners who call in to participate in the live broadcast. An average charge is between $19 and $29. Incentives are frequently offered to generate interest, such as a free report to download when they enroll.

2. Because many teleseminars offered by the masses are available free of charge, you may decide to offer your first event at no cost. Depending on the subject matter and industry, however, you may be able to charge a fee for participation. Research how other companies within your field, if any, conduct seminars by phone. Do they believe the information is worth buying? If so, charge a fee. If not, you can still move forward to record and sell your information.

3. Record and sell the teleseminar. The preferred recording method starts by choosing an online conference calling firm and setting up a free account. Once done, you receive your own conference teleseminar telephone number and code for participants to call on the day and time your event is scheduled. You also receive an additional code to key into your telephone that identifies you as the conference host. When the teleseminar is complete, your account includes access to a downloadable recording for distribution in whatever format you wish. All of this is free of cost unless your local telephone company charges you for minutes used on your land line (corded) or cell phone during the call.

4. Make the teleseminar transcript available by mail or e-mail for anyone who wants a text copy. Some people prefer text rather than a recording. The script is another product sold alongside the CD.

5. Once you finalize your teleseminar, you'll ask yourself why it took so long to start. You'll appreciate its simplicity and begin searching for new participants in collaborations and interviews. Best of all, you'll build an intellectual property library as well as a network of followers who look forward to hearing your next teleseminar.

> Look up the term "conference call services" in a search engine to find companies that allow you to record teleseminars free of charge.

Teleseminar Preparations

Here are the steps to prepare and market your teleseminar:

1. *Decide on the topic.* Start with something easy. Subjects can be as simple as "Ten Ways to Safely Whiten Your Teeth" or "Twelve Tips to Find a Safe, Affordable Day Care Center." The chosen number featured within the title (five, eight, fifty,

etc.) isn't important. What matters is that you deliver information that listeners value in exchange for their investment.

2. *Choose the format.* Is it better for you to be the featured speaker, conduct the interview, or have someone ask you questions? Do you want to be considered the expert, or is it better to be viewed as an expert interviewer? Do you want to share the spotlight or be the star? Once you decide on the format, you can create the teleseminar's structure.

3. *Invite another person or persons to participate if others are part of your format.* Once she agrees to the interview, brief her about the subject matter, how long the teleseminar will run (60 minutes is average, 80 minutes is the maximum CD recording time), and the recording date. This will ensure open communication to keep both of you on track.

4. *Write a script.* How wonderful it would be if both of you could talk for an hour, maintaining focus and clarity about the subject, with no pauses and few mistakes. That won't happen unless a script is prepared in advance. A script ensures that the participants stay focused and the teleseminar contains only the most-valuable details. It also minimizes the number of recorded *ums* and *aahs.* Extemporaneous discussions not in the script are a refreshing addition. The host and guest are encouraged to share stories that complement the subject and play on each other's chemistry, especially if a point within the script reminds you of relevant facts you wish to share with listeners. Writing a script is the most time-consuming process for this project whether recording the teleseminar alone or with others. A good script consists of questions and answers or information to be shared by both parties. It also includes a minimum of two pauses, one at midpoint and another at the end. It's the point where marketing is added, informing the listener about your respective expertise, website URLs, and telephone numbers (phone numbers aren't needed if website addresses are provided). When the script is complete, it is reviewed by both parties and edited if needed. The recording can now proceed at the set date and time through the company with whom you have an online conference call account.

5. *Begin marketing the teleseminar through appropriate methods,* which may include tweets through Twitter, postings on your business's Facebook page, electronic newsletter (more details on this later in the chapter), and a series of e-mails sent directly to followers through your e-mail marketing account.

Using a calendar, create a schedule to determine when notifications will be sent through each chosen method to ensure that everyone knows and is reminded about the upcoming teleseminar.

6. *Call the telephone number given to you by the conference recording company at least five minutes before the teleseminar begins.* Have water and mints nearby. Today's more-stable technology allows you to use either a land line phone or cell phone for the recording. When the time arrives, greet your listeners, and begin delivering value.

7. When the event ends, the recording company will provide you with the code to download your teleseminar for distribution to anyone who registered for the event but was not able to listen live.

8. *Listen to the recording when possible.* Be excited, not fearful, of hearing your voice and, if recorded with others, the chemistry between you and collaborators. Remember that you are an expert with a message to share with people who want to hear your ideas, solutions, and advice.

Target market definition: www.entrepreneur.com/encyclopedia/term/82498 .html

---

9. *Continue to market the teleseminar* through print marketing materials, your website or blog, online newsletters, social media, and collaborations with colleagues and other associates. The goal is to tell everyone within the target market that your teleseminar is available and why it benefits them to get it now.

Marketing materials encourage sales by sharing the teleseminar's highlights. Here's the partial text for a marketing teleseminar I recorded with a colleague:

Hear this lively fifty-minute CD covering six months of savvy marketing techniques. You'll learn:

When and where to create special occasion promotions.
How to capitalize on little-known events that generate sales.
Why ethnic occasions are important and which ones to promote.

Which products and services encourage year-round loyalty.

Where to sell products and services to "captive" audiences.

Information extracted from the teleseminar for marketing purposes answers the question, "What's in it for me to register for or buy this product?" Answering that one question encourages subscriptions for the live event as well as continuous sales.

Telephone Receiver or Headphone?

My recording experience reveals that a headphone attachment not only provides better clarity, it also keeps your hands free to turn script pages or access a computer during the teleseminar.

Recording Costs and Projected Revenues

Taping a teleseminar costs more in time than money. Any associated costs are charged by your local telephone company if you are charged for minutes. You will also pay for blank CDs and postage if you duplicate recordings with your computer and send the CDs to customers by mail. The low expense not only creates a powerful revenue generator but also markets your expertise in two formats—in text (transcript) and teleseminar format (CD). Both products generate sales all year as long as you continue to market. Don't be surprised if competitors begin offering a similar product to their customers. Just make sure that you continue to collaborate with experts who recognize and appreciate the product's value to a worldwide audience.

If duplicating the teleseminar recording on your computer is not possible or practical, CD duplicating companies will perform the work. Some companies offer first-time specials, while others will duplicate a minimum of one at a time. These companies will also label and package the teleseminar, leaving you with time to find new ways to create and sell new teleseminar subjects that deliver results to listeners and revenue to your bank account.

Directories

Individuals, groups, and corporations require many types of information. Some are available in books and e-books, and other forms are found on the Internet. People search for compilations created by resourceful firms because they are not in the position to gather the details on their own. Information seekers want one concise list that saves them time and energy. This is why directories on every conceivable subject are popular products that we solo business owners organize and sell.

Think about this: You frequently receive calls and e-mails asking for industry information. You've been referring other companies' products and services for months with no referral fee if a sale is transacted. The only way for you to profit from your knowledge is to create reference materials that list the types of resources callers request most. Such materials will turn your knowledge into a marketable product.

Here's a sample of requested information:

- Wholesalers of specific resources
- Statistics for niche industries
- Distributors of wholesale or retail services
- Resource listings for hard-to-find products
- Products or services located in specific states, regions, or countries

Directories are quick to compile and update on a yearly basis, especially when you participate in the industry that gives you access to the data. You can market the availability of the data in different formats, such as:

- Text by e-mail
- Downloadable PDF by e-mail
- CD by mail
- Text by mail

Because of its simplicity, directories seem to be an underappreciated product in terms of creation, but it is a valuable commodity in all industries. In some cases you will have to perform additional research to complete a directory. However, your insider knowledge makes the data easy to find.

My first directory was a listing of gift industry shows throughout the United States. I created it because of the daily telephone calls and e-mails I received asking me for this material. Each interruption costs time, usually ten to twenty minutes. I realized the monetary potential and created a directory listing worldwide industry shows. Thousands were sold for $29.95 in text format. Now that a downloadable version is available, I sell many more.

Deciding Which Directories to Create

Consider creating directories that are simple to compile yet difficult or time consuming for people or groups outside of your industry to collect on their own. Groups include the media, organizations that require specialized products or services, and individuals who are new to your industry.

As you start the process, consider the details you are asked to provide when callers use your company as a "411" service. That's the information to begin compiling. Most requests are for the following:

- Business name
- Address
- Regular and toll-free numbers
- Website URL and e-mail address
- Brief product or service description

It can also include:

- Contact name
- Credit cards accepted
- Minimum order quantity or minimum dollar amount for purchases
- Other industry-standard details

Directories display source information in a manner that's easy to understand. This is how a listing might be created for one type of directory.

The ABC Company	V ❑	Minimum Order: $100
123 Main Drive	MC ❑	
Buffalo, NY 15259	AX ❑	
Toll-free: (800) 555-1212	DISC ❑	
Fax: (800) 555-1213		
www.abccomp.com		**Galvanized tubes and wires**

Here's similar information compiled in another format on the next page.

The ABC Company
123 Main Drive
Buffalo, NY 15259
Toll-free: (800) 555-1212
Fax: (800) 555-1213
www.abccomp.com
Galvanized tubes and wires

In the first example, the directory shows a structure arranged in a space-saving two- or three-column format. The second example allows the right side of the page to remain blank for note taking.

Not all customers want every detail about companies within your industry. Some directories require the long version, while others provide a quick sketch of industry information. Clients' questions will help you put the best-selling formats together.

Directories elevate your status as an expert because industry compilations are often created by insiders who collect this material for their own use. Because these details are important to you and contained in a database management program, the idea occurs that the same information may be beneficial to others. Your insider knowledge turns material you consult on a daily basis into a marketable product.

Web Videos

Creating a video about your product or service, then posting and promoting it on your website or popular video-sharing community, is easier than you imagine. The simplest way to begin producing videos is to first choose the equipment that will record your message. Choices include:

- Camera
- Camcorder
- Cell phone camera
- Web camera, also known as a webcam

Many entrepreneurs add video recording equipment to their marketing arsenal because allowing prospects to see a visual message or providing clients with help through a video tutorial is a powerful sales tool. Video creation elevates your firm above all competitors who do not utilize video in their marketing. The quickest method to start the process is through a webcam or camcorder although a traditional camera or cell phone camera are substitutes until one of the first two options are purchased.

A webcam is usually mounted above your computer's monitor or built within a laptop computer or tablet. Its position allows you to be in front of the camera to record your motions while speaking to the audience. If there's no need for you to walk from one room to another while speaking, a webcam may work to your advantage. However, if your message is best created similar to a movie, conducting interviews, or through multiple scenes, a camcorder is the more appropriate option.

There's a cost for each product, from an average of $49 for an external webcam to $300 or more for a camcorder, depending on the model and manufacturer. Accessories may also be required, such as lighting to brighten the scene and a tripod to hold the camcorder steadily. The investment is worth the money as long as you've set goals to grow your business through this medium.

Limit each video's length to no more than three to five minutes, except in cases where you're teaching a course or conducting a seminar. Individuals who watch videos prefer information delivered quickly. Their patience can wane, so get to the point as fast as possible. Consider creating a series of videos as an introduction to or a promotion of your for-sale products.

Webcams and camcorders are sold with their own instruction manual. Follow it to install the product and verify its compatibility with your computer. The most taxing yet fulfilling part comes next: creating videos with your equipment as you prepare the finished product for Internet promotion. This step will take some time to master, and no doubt you'll feel the urge to do everything right the first time. That's highly unlikely. As you work on this project, remember the phrase, "You only get one chance to make a first impression." It will take several attempts to record a session that you're proud to show on the web.

My first computer experience was completed after sixteen tapings. At that point I grew tired of trying to live up to my inflated expectations and simply put together a three-minute video that I knew would please the audience.

It's much easier today to upload (transfer your video from the recording device to the computer and then to the Internet) then when video first became popular.

1. Follow the directions provided by your device's instruction guide to upload your video from the device to your computer. This is done so you can watch the video on your monitor before uploading it onto the Internet and also to save the video in case you want to access the original recording. The instructions will also guide you if edits to the recording are required.

2. Make sure your video is in a format accepted by your preferred video sharing sites (the most-popular host is YouTube.com explained in chapter 2). Universal formats (also known as extensions) include .avi, .mp3, and mp4. If your video does not include an acceptable extension, it's wise to convert the video before uploading it to the sharing site. Converting your video is done with one of the many free conversion programs found on the Internet.

3. Upload the video directly to YouTube.com or the video-sharing site you prefer. You'll open a free account on the chosen site before uploading your video to your account. Once your videos are added, the video-sharing site (which is now your video's host) will provide you with coding to place a still picture of the video clip on your website, blog, or in any environment that allows visitors to click and watch the video.

The number of video-sharing sites increases every day. Consult a search engine to broaden your choices. Also look at competitive websites to learn which service they use. You'll usually find the video host's name at the top or bottom of the screen that surrounds the recording. YouTube is the default Internet host because as a solo marketer, it's wise to make your videos available on a high-traffic site. If you choose to create videos seen only by clients rather than the general public, YouTube offers a method for private screening, and Amazon.com's Simple Storage Service (S3) has grown in popularity as a place for video storage for public and private viewing.

Consider recording videos at least twice a month to keep your growing audience watching and listening to your message.

Creating videos costs you time and/or money, but the additional promotion and revenue generated through this visual medium makes the investment worthwhile.

Amazon S3: http://aws.amazon.com/s3/

Web Radio

In 2001 Excite.com allowed web visitors to create their own free, online radio show. A microphone was required. The website let you post the date and time of your broadcast on the Excite.com radio show's home page for the world to see twenty-four hours a day. This was revolutionary. I wrote a press release about my groundbreaking show, which still exists in web archives. I also promoted information about the broadcast on my website.

Sample radio show press release: www.prweb.com/releases/2001/6/prweb25917.htm

---

Excite.com canceled the broadcasting area just weeks after I started using it, but the experience gave me an introduction to a marketing tool that attracts web listeners and still does so today.

Online radio shows discuss many topics, and the broadcasting technology is still in development. There's lots of room for growth, which is good for home-based and solo business owners ready to market their products and services through online shows created with audio technology.

Is Online Radio for You?

Radio show creation is open to every solo business owner, but some of us will not add this to our marketing. Some business owners work in industries where prospects and clients have no time or interest in listening to an online broadcast. They prefer reading text, watching a video, getting updates through a social media page, or visiting a website. Any of these options can turn clients into online radio fans, allowing you to educate and inform through this verbal medium. Here are two possibilities:

- There are at least a dozen experts you can count on to interview, and online radio is the place to generate industry interest and get clients and fans listening and asking questions as part of the show's format.
- New and exciting events frequently occur in your industry, and a method to bring that news to your audience is by radio in a voice that mimics the marketing of a tell-all book or grocery store magazine.

> **Blog Talk Radio:** www.blogtalkradio.com

If you market to an audience that's on the go, that prefers listening to information through a computer, or that downloads one-to-one interviews to portable devices, then it's time to consider communicating with your own online radio show. Here's how to proceed:

1. Give your show a catchy name. The title describes the content so that listeners recognize your expertise before they tune in.

2. Determine the show's length, format, and frequency. Professional broadcasters stay within preset boundaries, and following that model will work for you. Choose a length from twenty to forty-five minutes, a format that uses one host (you) or a host and guest, and a weekly or monthly production timetable. These are reasonable strategies for the first-time radio show host.

3. Research the competition. Do other radio shows on your topic exist? If so, make a list of them and the formats they follow, using the points under step 2 as a guide. Resist canceling your show just because someone else hosts a similar program. There's room for you as well.

4. Record multiple shows consecutively. Just because your show is broadcast once a week or month doesn't mean that's it's live. For efficiency's sake, plan and produce several shows at the same time.

5. Invite industry suppliers to sponsor your radio show. Firms often search for new methods to reach customers. Help them to understand how partnering with you to distribute the show will increase their exposure to new and familiar audiences.

Read and understand all information available about creating, launching, and maintaining your radio show before you begin. Research is part of Janet Green's marketing plan in chapter 1 as she is temporarily more comfortable speaking on air than on stage. Most of all, ask yourself: "How will this resource enhance my marketing plan?" The answer sets in motion a well-defined model to grow an audience that tunes in regularly and considers you as the leading authority in your field.

E-books

The popularity of Kindle, Nook, iPad, and comparable devices caused a surge in e-book creation, making authors of anyone with expert advice or fictional tales to share with the world. An electronic book (e-book) was once made by typing text into a Microsoft Word file and converting that text into a PDF document for delivery by e-mail. It was sent to anyone ordering it mainly as a bonus for visiting a website, subscribing to an electronic newsletter, or ordering a product or service. This type of e-book is still popular, easy to publish, and distributed for these and other reasons, so let's start there.

> **E-book definition:** http://on.wsj.com/aOchuP

Before devices came on the scene, the word *e-book* described any type of document (special report, industry tips, how-to manual, etc.) made and distributed online and rarely, though sometimes available, printed as a traditional book. At year's end many solo business owners who operate blogs chose a number of posts for re-styling into an e-book delivered by e-mail to their clients as a bonus or appreciation for their business. Here's how this is done:

1. Decide on the information to compile. As mentioned, the text can come from your blog, a series of articles written by you in the past but no longer available online, frequently asked questions and responses based on speeches or consultations, or other text that is considered as valuable and marketable content. You can also include photographic images as a complement.

2. Format the content and images in Word with landscape as the paper orientation and margins set at 0.8" on all sides. This format allows readers to see one page at a time on a computer monitor without scrolling down to access the rest of the page. The number of content pages is a minimum of 8 and average of 24 though the e-book can be longer.

3. Add headers and footers similar to a traditional book, and add your biography and any disclaimers at the end. Review the format and text for clarity before converting the document into PDF format.

4. Select a PDF converter to format the e-book for proper viewing. You'll find many free converters through search engine research.

5. Save the document, upload it to your website, blog, or social media account for distribution. Test the document's delivery before announcing its availability.

While this e-book-creation and distribution method is still acceptable, the launch of the Kindle device by Amazon.com forever changed what's known as e-book technology because today's standard makes everyone an author without acceptance by traditional publishers.

The delivery described above is one where the e-book is a marketing tool with no cost expected from the receiver. Today's e-book is created for technological devices and range from 99 cents and up in price for digital delivery. These self-published authors can elect to distribute their product free of charge as a one-day special or always make the material fee based. Such e-books include an average of 48 pages and are rated by readers in the same manner as traditional books.

Written tutorials, videos, and webinar demonstrations are available online on sites such as www.ColorYourLifePublished.com and explain the entire e-book process, including how to establish accounts with Amazon.com and BarnesAndNoble.com to upload your e-books into their systems for purchase by buyers who read your marketing messages through online and offline channels.

This technology is still new and open for your exploration. There's a good chance that books in your industry are not yet available or popular as e-books, and you can accomplish this project and market it to the masses, leading them to your online real estate for more information.

Membership Sites

You now know about six marketing methods open to you, all of interest to prospects and clients in whatever form they prefer. What if all of this information was available in one place online in a community you control? Membership communities are becoming popular sites to join online bringing professionals, parents, sports enthusiasts, and other like-minded people together in one space.

A membership site allows you to deliver resources you don't want available free of charge in an area that's restricted to people that pay a monthly or yearly fee for access. It can produce a healthy income if your business is a niche category where information about the product or service isn't readily accessible because of the industry or profession.

There are lots of options for membership site creation depending on your target market. Home schooling, cooking, and traveling are just some topics online today as membership communities. Roger Green can create a site specifically for Charlotte-based golfers who require insider tips on golfing at area clubs or can access tickets for upcoming events that cannot be found or purchased elsewhere. Janet Green's teleseminar tips on financial planning and interviews with well-known financial experts are resources to launch her membership site.

Now that you realize the potential for product and service businesses, consider whether a membership site is in your future. Reviewing the information shared in this chapter, your members might receive:

- Teleseminars and webinars about little-known or rarely-discussed industry or professional solutions.
- Directories featuring information for industry resources that aren't compiled elsewhere.
- Private videos of demonstrations, interviews with industry leaders, and tours of favorite locations.
- Weekly audios that discuss how-to information in a step-by-step format.
- E-books that reveal new resources in text and photographic content.

Membership site technology is still in its infancy. You'll find several companies online that are leaders in this field with various pricing and services available either for a lifetime after purchase or on a monthly basis. Don't let low costs sway you to choose one membership site program over another. As with all decisions, it's important to research which program:

- Is as easy to set up as creating a website or blog without the need to know HTML or other coding.
- Offers its own community or forum to troubleshoot site problems, and which of those communities include frequent responses from the software maker's staff.
- Includes software updates performed at least once a year that are either free or available for a nominal fee.

- Allows integration of popular programs for e-mail marketing and payment purposes.
- Is customizable so you can create an attractive site and easily deliver resources to members.

You may not be ready to create a membership site. However, keep this option on the radar to expand both your intellectual property holdings and client list.

Most marketers will try one or two of the easiest options first, not all of the ideas at once. Apply that strategy yourself, keeping track of results and moving forward to gain new customers who trust your opinion and depend on your expertise.

The following worksheet helps you decide which of these technological tools are right for your firm.

Marketing Products under Consideration Worksheet

(Place checkmarks where appropriate)

Marketing Product	Integrate into Plan Now	Consider at a Later Date	Not a Good Fit	Other Comments
Teleseminars				
Webinars				
Directories				
Web Videos				
Web Radio				
E-books				
Membership Sites				

07 Internet Help to the Rescue

The media talk as if every business on the planet operates a website. But that isn't true. If you are part of the group that doesn't yet have an Internet presence, is it too late to create a web identity? Not at all, and it's time to begin your journey establishing a presence on the web.

You may have tried to create an Internet site in the past, or perhaps someone was supposed to help you get online, but things didn't work out. Opportunities for getting online have changed for the better, so you'll be able to get a site up and running on your own. At the very least you'll know your options and be able to move forward with this important element of running and marketing a business.

Getting on the web is affordable these days. I created my first website in 1997 when the technology was in its infancy. At that time maintaining my site cost me $1,170 per year; now it costs $80, and that includes a shopping cart and blogging capabilities, two subjects explored later in this chapter. Some web hosts (the companies that keep your website visible on the Internet) provide service for less than the $80 I pay. This chapter will help you find reputable companies at an affordable cost.

At the end of this chapter, you'll be ready to create an online presence, notify search engines of your address, and focus on bringing visitors to your virtual door.

> **Web host definition:** http://bit.ly/UzZS68

In a nutshell, the five steps you'll take to get online and market your site's existence are:

1. Choose a website name and register it with an Internet registration company.
2. Research website hosts, weighing each company's benefits. Then decide on a host provider.
3. Select a web creation software package. The easiest choices are: a host that makes customizable, online templates available; choosing a blog as your primary website; bypassing the web host's templates in favor of web page software.
4. Review industry-based websites to determine strengths and weaknesses. Look at websites outside of your industry for ideas to make your site a place that visitors return to often.
5. Determine the best methods to create awareness, increase site traffic, track visitors, and capture sales.

Let's look at these five steps in detail.

Step 1: Select and Register Your Website's Name

A website name is the address that online users type into an Internet browser to find information about a particular industry, hobby, news event, and thousands of other topics. The site's address is known in technological terms as a uniform resource locator, or URL. Your first choice for a business-related URL is the actual name of your business. One of my companies, Sweet Survival, uses the web address www.SweetSurvival.com. The name was available at the time of registration. Another choice is to register your own name. I registered the URL www.ShirleyGeorgeFrazier.com. When individuals are searching for information on me, that's the first address they will consider typing into their Internet browser. Millions of web names have been claimed, and many are being registered as you read this book. However, don't let that deter you from researching and claiming your preferred URL.

> **Uniform resource locator (URL) definition:** http://bit.ly/RntXsW

Another smart option that we home-based business owners choose is to register name differentiations and extensions. A company such as Coca-Cola may choose to protect its brand by registering the Coca-Cola URL with .com, .net, and .org, the top three extensions of choice for name registration. These choices are also open to you as you select registration names for your site.

In time you may find that registering multiple extensions and name variations isn't worth the cost, but it's wise to consider doing so at the beginning. Later on you can determine whether to continue paying for the additional names or to drop them.

If the name you desire is taken, registration firms will suggest other options, including hyphens between words (www.your-web-name.com), the letter "e" (electronic) in front of the name (www.eyourwebname.com), and the word "online" at the end of the name (www.yourwebnameonline.com).

Another possible web name is one based on the product or service you sell. My site Sweet Survival is the place where individuals learn about starting a gift basket business. Visitors can find the site by typing the URL www.SweetSurvival.com, or they can use the alternate address, www.GiftBasketBusiness.com. The latter is easier for most people to remember, as it focuses on the site's purpose. The memorability of a name is something to consider when searching for a web name and alternate URLs.

A URL in any format other than the choices mentioned above is an outdated format not in your best interest. Your site's name is to follow the pattern "www.yoursitename .com" rather than www.yoursitename.hostname.com, which is the only option for registering a site at some of the free hosting sites.

Who Registers URL Names?

There are many domain name registrants on the Internet. The most popular and best-known companies are NetworkSolutions.com, Register.com, and GoDaddy. com. Go online to check the availability of and registration for your preferred URL. You will see price differences between the companies, but don't assume that a lower-priced company is less useful than higher-priced ones. All of them register URLs in the same manner and on the same level.

Network Solutions and Register.com charge $34.99 and $38.00 per year, respectively, to register your website name, while GoDaddy.com charges approximately $13.00 per year. All three offer the same registration service. When visiting each site, you will also find a host of services that can be bundled with name registration, such as web hosting, access to additional e-mail boxes, and search engine submission assistance. You can pay for services through these firms, or you can look for another host that provides lots of website space, e-mail capabilities, blogging tools, and more for similar or lower costs than the three companies named here.

Step 2: Research Host Sites

Which companies will provide you with the most in service and amenities for the best price? As you research sites, complete the Web Host Comparison Worksheet to help identify web hosts with the best deal for the features you desire. Here are the services and features that most solo and home-based business owners request:

- Website storage space of 10 gigabytes (GB) and up.

Gigabyte definition: www.techterms.com/definition/gigabyte

- A minimum of ten e-mail boxes (many hosts are generous, providing twenty or more). Most businesses need multiple e-mail boxes so that each box can be used for a different function or service (help@yourwebname.com, orders@yourwebname.com, yourname@yourwebname.com, etc.).
- A secure shopping cart to sell an unlimited amount of products and services. Some web hosts provide access to one shopping cart, while others give you five or more carts that are customizable with your logo, product or service photos, and the ability to collect payments through credit cards and alternative payment collectors, along with other amenities.
- The options to create a site using the host's built-in templates, or a site set up as a blog, which is also part of the host's system.
- Visitor tracking support through internal web statistics. Most if not all hosts provide detailed statistics on the numbers of website visitors, how they found you, and which pages they visit. If everything else is adequate through your preferred host, statistics can be gathered through free, online sources such as the popular Google Analytics that use charts and forms to provide a complete, statistical picture.

- Service on request. No web host is worth the price if you are unable to get support by telephone or e-mail when you have questions or concerns about your web hosting plan or specific features. A good host will make a frequently asked questions (FAQ) area available on its site to answer general queries. However, you'll want to contact a live person by phone or expect a prompt response by e-mail if a problem occurs that isn't addressed in the FAQs.

Unfortunately, you won't know if you've chosen a web host with good service until you need to contact customer support, and by then you've already signed on as a client. One way to find a good web host is to ask colleagues about their host experiences. Another is to consult social media and message boards on the Internet for opinions, taking what you read with a grain of salt, knowing that one individual who is dissatisfied is not representative of everyone hosted through that firm.

Web Host Comparison Worksheet

NAME OF HOST				
FEATURES	Host 1	Host 2	Host 3	Host 4
Setup fees (yes or no)				
Monthly or yearly cost				
Available number of subdomains				
(alternate web names that can be linked				
to the main URL)				
Amount of available web space (in gigabytes)				
Number of e-mail accounts				
Spam filtering?				
Virus scanning?				
Blogging capabilities (yes or no)				
Shopping cart with SSL protection (yes or no)				
Statistics capabilities (yes or no)				
Internal firewall protection				
(site security on their servers) (yes or no)				
On-site tutorials (yes or no)				
24/7 support (yes or no)				
By telephone?				
By e-mail?				

Step 3: Select Website Creation Software

There were few industry competitors in my field when I created my first site in 1997. I chose Microsoft FrontPage software to design the site because I read about its ease of use and the fact that it didn't require web coding knowledge, also known as HTML. Still, I anticipated a steep learning curve and didn't look forward to understanding a new language just to create a website.

The hosting company I chose offered a shopping cart, which I customized for receiving orders online. But the cart wasn't secure from access to credit card numbers by unscrupulous people. I had to apply to an outside firm to add an SSL certificate that encrypted each client's credit card number when entered into my cart. When orders arrived, I processed the credit card information through a terminal in my office. This in-office terminal had been set up with help from my bank years before I established an online presence. I used my printer to print the order from the computer and manually processed the transaction.

Hypertext markup language (HTML): www.merriam-webster.com/dictionary/html

Secure socket layer (SSL): http://bit.ly/d5uYwC

That office procedure ended years ago for me because better choices exist today, and they're also available for you. Today there are online payment solutions and smartphone processing systems that handle transactions. This streamlines the order processing and places the funds, minus transaction fees, into the bank account of your choice.

I was pleasantly surprised with my web page software experience and am just as pleased that today's website hosts make templates available. This allows you to get up and running on the web much quicker than it took years ago.

Web hosts not only broadcast your website on the Internet, they also provide the tools to create a site that's informative, interesting, and attractive. No more "under construction" signs or blank home pages announcing your forthcoming site. Choose a web host, receive your user name and password by e-mail within minutes after sign-up, and follow the host's instructions to begin creating a site.

In most cases you'll be given the choice by your host to create your pages as a traditional website or as a blog. Either choice is acceptable, depending on the structure you want and tools that are required to showcase what you have to offer visitors. There's one main difference. A blog turns each text entry on your web pages into a communication device, allowing visitors to insert comments. You can, however, turn off the ability to comment either immediately or days after each article is posted on the blog. A traditional website does not provide that capability.

Popular blog programs: Blogger www.blogger.com; WordPress www.wordpress.org

Both traditional websites and blogs can be set up with narrow columns on the left and/or right side of each page. These columns are called sidebars. Here is where you add a site's table of contents and other links to valuable information on the site.

You can also create your site by using web page software purchased through online sellers or downloaded from the manufacturer's computer to yours. This software has been available for as long as the Internet has existed. Although online templates are popular website-making choices, software will continue to play a role in site creation and be chosen by individuals who either have familiarity with the product or feel more comfortable working with it.

Microsoft Expression Studio (FrontPage no longer exists) and Adobe Dreamweaver (formerly owned by Macromedia) are said to be easy-to-use software packages. Because the templates provided by web hosts are so simple to arrange, it is wise to work with them first if you're not familiar with website software.

Web page software: Microsoft Expression Studio http://www.microsoft.com/expression/; Adobe Dreamweaver www.adobe.com/products/dreamweaver.html

Most software today is not accompanied by a manual explaining how to install and use the product. That leads many users to consult easy-to-understand tutorials available online and in books from libraries and bookstores. Do not hesitate to review these additional sources for help.

Setting Up Your Shopping Cart

The ability to link a shopping cart to a site, offering customers a way to pay online for goods and services, was once a cost over and above the initial website investment. This circumstance has changed for the better. Web hosts now offer shopping carts with basic web services. These carts are licensed to web hosts, allowing users to take advantage of a cart's encrypted technology to add whatever you sell while capturing the buyer's personal information and credit card number. PayPal.com also makes selling and collecting monies online easy. Once you set up a business account with PayPal and designate your preferred bank account to transfer monies from sales, you also have access to tools to create your own shopping cart through PayPal's service. Visit their site for more information.

> **PayPal business accounts:** www.paypal.com/webapps/mpp/merchant/

Some carts are still not totally customizable. There are times when you must manually adjust shipping costs applied to an order when it arrives in your in-box, but most other functions are controllable.

You aren't necessarily locked into using your web host's cart, especially if another type of cart seems to be a better solution for the items you sell. Perhaps you sell reports that are downloaded and delivered directly by e-mail after a customer pays. Instead of manually processing the order in your office and physically sending the report through your computer, you can find an online service whose shopping cart handles the online report delivery and places the revenue into the bank account of your choice, minus fees. If this streamlined method is for you, carts exist that make selling a hands-free process.

Most of all, online shopping carts are evolving as quickly as the Internet, and that's good news for us home-based owners with lots of projects and limited time.

Step 4: Review Other Websites

There's no doubt that other people in your industry have set up sites on the web. Your mission is to locate your industry partners and competitors, bookmarking their sites so that you can review them meticulously to uncover their strengths and weaknesses. This will help you to decide what's best to include on your site and how to move forward adding that information.

No two websites are alike, even when they're part of the same industry or address the same topic. That's why looking at sites that are outside of your industry gives you a well-rounded focus on what may work to make your site a unique place that piques visitors' interest and brings them back to see what's new.

Consider websites that you bookmark as part of your favorites. What makes those sites special enough for bookmarking, and how can you add that ingenuity to your forthcoming site?

Hopefully, you already have a vision regarding your site structure and layout. Here's a list of pages to consider creating as you get ready to put your business on the Internet.

Home page. Includes an introduction to the site, reason why the site is a primary source for goods and services on a particular topic, and summary of what visitors will find on subsequent pages.

"What's new" page. Announces recent updates on the site that visitors may not know exist.

Frequently asked questions page. Contains basic questions and answers about your business, its policies and terms of service, and general information about the industry in which you participate.

Products and services page. Provides information on items and/or consulting help made available to site visitors.

Articles or tips pages. A document or documents, written in a long or short format by you or another knowledgeable party, that educates visitors on industry details that make your product or service valuable.

Newsletter subscription page. Allows and encourages visitors to subscribe to your online weekly or monthly publication.

Different types of information are critical to every business website, and these six pages begin to mold your site into a place where expert material and advice are found by individuals looking for ideas and solutions.

Use photographs, graphic images, audios, and videos as frequently as required to make your site interesting and attractive.

As you decide on your website's structure, try not to become overwhelmed by the options. You don't want an unorganized site with pages that confuse and repel visitors. Choose a few strong options at the outset and keep other opportunities in mind. In the coming years you'll change the site's template and structure to reflect the content that visitors want most. On-site and informal surveys will help you uncover how to make your site a magnet, attracting worldwide visitors who look to you for news, ideas, and products that benefit them.

Step 5: Create Site Buzz on a Budget

Making individuals aware of your website is a matter of persistence. You may complete many objectives within a week to let people know you exist. However, it will take many more days—or months—to get the publicity train up to speed. The easiest methods you can put into place immediately are:

1. Creating awareness by submitting your site to search engines.
2. Increasing site traffic by leaving your signature on sites where people want to know more about your expertise.
3. Tracking website visitors (where they come from and where they migrate on your site).
4. Capturing sales by convincing visitors about the benefits of products and services.

Creating Awareness

A good part of your research has been spent on the web looking at competitive sites, as mentioned earlier. Once you upload your site onto the web, you'll want to contact the major search engines about your presence.

There are hundreds of search engines on the web, but only contact Google, Yahoo!, and Bing, the three sites that lead all others. Type "submit your site to (name of search site)" in any search engine to find the pages for submission, and follow the directions. This is the procedure whether you maintain a website or blog.

Submitting your site's URL to search engines begins the task of search engine optimization (SEO). This crucial part of website or blog maintenance allows search engines to recognize your site's existence and categorize its focus according to information on each page.

Search engine definition: http://bit.ly/TNVDmo

Every website and blog template includes a line in your account's administrative area to list keywords for each page. For example, if your business is interior decorating, you will create pages on your site featuring living room, kitchen, and man cave makeovers. Each of those pages will contain keywords specific to the page's topic. Do not include keywords such as "man cave" and "pool table" on the page that features kitchen makeovers, or search engines will penalize the page for misleading search engine users who are looking for man cave information but find kitchen makeovers on the page.

Each of your website or blog pages is to include keywords specific to the content. Over time, factual page keywords move the page's position up in search engine ranking until it arrives on page one for those particular keywords, the holy grail of search engine optimization. Choose your keywords wisely, monitor each page's search engine ranking through online statistics, and your site may reach top status in its category.

Increasing Site Traffic

Another part of your research will uncover places where people are most likely interested in your site's focus. Such places include e-mail signatures, social media, and message boards.

E-mail Signatures

Most e-mail programs allow you to create a custom signature, also known as a SIG file, which appears each time you write or respond to an e-mail. This signature is a call to action about something relevant you wish to share with individuals, convincing them to visit your site or blog, subscribe to a newsletter, sign up for a complimentary appointment, receive a free report, and promote other benefits to visitors.

Signature (SIG) definition: www.marketingterms.com/dictionary/sig_file/

A maximum of three links is appropriate within a custom e-mail signature. It's enough to give visitors a glimpse into what you offer and not so much that confusion stops them from clicking on the highlighted links.

Here's a sample signature found at the end of an e-mail message:

Gift Basket Business

Where designers learn, grow, and profit

www.GiftBasketBusiness.com

Join us on Facebook for tips, ideas, solutions

www.facebook.com/GiftBasketBusiness

Ph: 555-555-5555 | Skype: shirleyfrazier

Follow me on Twitter @BasketSupplies

Look for the custom signature link within your e-mail program. Create your own signature, reviewing and refining it until your high-value message is complete.

Social Media

Twitter, Facebook, and LinkedIn, the popular social media sites mentioned in chapter 2, allow you to share information that reveal your insights, wisdom, and a way for others who read your comments to learn who you are and what you do.

Twitter users who are intrigued with you due to re-tweets by your followers will visit your website as long as the site's URL is posted in your Twitter description. You can increase visitors to your Facebook business page by finding and commenting on competitive Facebook pages as well as posting comments on pages belonging to popular people, brands, and industry leaders. LinkedIn's structure lets you participate in conversations by asking business questions and answering questions posted by other members.

Make time to post comments or respond to questions that you can easily answer at a time that's convenient to your schedule, or you'll find yourself minding other people's business rather than tending to your own.

Message Boards

A signature at the end of a message board post is similar to an e-mail SIG file. It may be shorter than the one shown above, but it's usually not longer. Like the e-mail signature, the message board end signature is meant to provide readers with additional information about what's on your site.

In both cases this self-serving message is more informational than advertorial. Savvy website surfers know the difference between both and are more apt to click on the link if it leads to a source that shares information rather than tries to sell a product or service. Not all signature creators follow this rule, but it's best to do so to develop trust with other posters, especially if you are a frequent message-board participant.

Tracking Visitors

One of the most important ways to bring visitors to your site and keep them coming back is to know how they found your site in the first place. Did they arrive through a link at another site? Did a news report featuring your website cause the connection? Did someone click on a link you added to a message board or in social media? You won't always know the exact answer, but there will be signs that point you in the right direction to learn how your site was found.

Site analytics programs reveal how people find you on the web. These statistical programs for your website tell you which pages visitors reviewed and the length of each visit. The programs let you capitalize on site traffic and understand the hot-button issues, articles, products, and overall content that interest visitors.

Analytics programs reveal many types of data about your site, including:

- How visitors access it (direct, web links, search engine, social media, etc.)
- The number of new visitors and returning visitors
- Pages on your site that are popular and pages that are not
- The number of visitors per day, week, month, and year
- The geographic location of site visitors (by US state or worldwide country)

Some statistics programs are basic, disclosing minimum information about site visitors, while others display extensive details in the form of charts and graphs. Program costs do not determine how deep the data are mined. There are many free programs that provide a wealth of statistical material. Type the words "analytics program" into a search engine to find tracking software that works for you.

These programs require that you add a line of coding to your website pages so that they can capture statistical information. This process is easy; most programs provide diagrams or instructions to help you add coding in the correct format. Today's free statistics programs don't require a link back to their site, nor do you need to add a large logo to your site in exchange for using the technology. Some programs require a small icon/logo, one that does not intrude on your website's real estate. Other programs, including the widely-popular Google Analytics, are undetectable on your site.

Finding Local and Online Support

The Internet is more than a place to connect with customers through your website, blog, or social media. It's also where you'll find help through professionals worldwide who can complete practically every task on your list. Outsourcing is a process that allows technical and administrative people to temporarily assist you with plan details that would otherwise slow your progress or keep you from completing tasks that are critical during the business start-up and growth phases.

Here's a short list of what outsource help (freelancers) can accomplish:

- Research your target market, local or worldwide competitors, industry books, and e-books
- Create your logo, marketing materials, website, or blog
- Write articles, newsletters, press releases
- Establish and monitor social media accounts
- Make telephone calls, set up and confirm appointments
- Monitor and answer your telephone
- Evaluate and create reports about your website or blog strengths and weaknesses
- Gather information for the creation of resource materials, reports, audio calls

How temporary help assists you and where they complete each task depends on your comfort level and work environment. If your office is small, with no room to allow another person to sit in your office, then virtual assistance is the preferred means of support. A virtual worker can exist anywhere in the world. Virtual helpers can complete most online projects. However, there are some tasks that a virtual assistant cannot handle, such as by-mail campaigns and entering original receipts into an accounting program. You will find that these independent workers can accomplish a lot more than the few things they're unable to perform.

Virtual Assistant

Virtual assistance is help you receive from a qualified person who completes work you assign in a place she sets up as her workspace outside of your office.

Several websites make it easy for you to find individuals with expert project assistance. These sites bring freelance workers together for you to post your job, explain what's involved, the time frame, and the price you'll pay per hour (for long-term assistance) or project (one-time support). Once enrolled on the site, you can post your job and terms. Individuals who qualify to complete the project contact you with their interest, and you choose a provider from all candidates. Finding help through outsourcing sites lets the site be your partner, ensuring that the freelancer is paid only after the work is completed to your satisfaction.

Virtual assistance help: www.elance.com; www.odesk.com; www.fiverr.com

If you prefer to hire a person who will work directly in your office, one source for assistance is an intern from a local college. Internships are available at most universities, facilitated through each department major. College counselors are happy to help connect you with a student whom you will train and pay either through college credits or a salary. Interns can also provide support as freelance workers outside of your office.

At-home moms, mature high school students, and individuals downsized from corporate jobs are three more groups who provide marketing assistance. No matter where you find suitable, qualified help, keep this strategy in mind to ensure that the interaction and results benefit everyone:

1. Write down a complete list of activities for the project so the helper understands the task, their role, time table, and expected results.
2. Pay a fair salary or fee for the assignment.
3. Be open to suggestions that freelancers express. They sometimes have a better strategy than yours.

4. Create a comfortable work environment for in-office workers including eating and lavatory areas that are not part of your family's personal space.

5. Include milestone checkpoints within the project, allowing you and the worker to review what's completed, upcoming steps, and concerns as the project progresses. Remember to commend the worker for continued or outstanding support.

As you work on business, start listing the tasks you perform that can be given to a virtual or in-office assistant. This will prepare you to hire help before overwhelm occurs.

Turning Visitors into Customers

Convincing prospects to take one step forward, from browsing your site to purchasing through the online shopping cart, takes just a few minutes for some visitors and weeks for others. Your site must be a combination of helpful information and influential text, providing enough of a comfort zone to put visitors at ease, elevating their trust level to buy your products and services.

What features convince visitors to trust you and place orders?

1. A money-back guarantee.
2. A prominently displayed business address, telephone number, and e-mail address for questions before or after the purchase.
3. A trial consultation (usually fifteen to twenty minutes).
4. Testimonials from satisfied customers.
5. Active presence on social media.
6. Evidence of your prominence and expertise, developed through years of industry participation.

Every business cannot offer all six "comfort factors," but two or three are often enough to get the sale. Review the online shopping benefits offered by your competition as posted in their printed literature and on their websites. Do competitors post none of these benefits? Then consider being first to offer them, which could sway their prospects to buy from you. Don't be surprised if the competition follows your lead, posting a list of benefits that mirrors or competes with your own.

Electronic Newsletters Keep Clients Connected

You've set up your website and installed a shopping cart. This is just the beginning of your journey to create an environment that clients and prospects visit often. After the initial launch, contact prospective visitors using postcards and other mailed literature as discussed in chapter 3. Another way to get their attention is to publish an electronic newsletter, which is interesting news you share with your subscribers combined with graphic images attractively arranged on a template provided to you by an online company that will distribute the newsletter by e-mail to your readers.

Electronic newsletters inform website visitors about your topic or industry and reasons for them to visit. This e-newsletter, as it's named on the Internet, contains news and ideas that appeal to readers. It is created using one of many templates provided by host firms specializing in e-newsletter creation and delivery to subscribers' e-mail addresses. The host firm also makes HTML code available so that people can subscribe to and unsubscribe from your publication. You also have access to statistics detailing the number of subscribers, how many e-newsletters were opened versus not opened, and which e-mail deliveries bounced.

Your e-newsletter format will depend on what subscribers want to read, and the same is true for its length. Some readers have time to absorb long newsletters, while others need short, concise publications that lead them back to more information found on your site. In many cases, the latter version is more valuable, since the purpose of a newsletter is to increase your website's readership and overall sales.

What type of information makes readers anticipate your e-newsletter?

- Original articles on your topic.
- Tips that readers can use immediately.
- Ideas generated by clients who ask questions by phone, e-mail, or through social media.

What details help you to market your business and sell to readers?

- Information on new products or services and where to find details on your site.
- Notification of items on sale in your online store.
- Links to hot topics being discussed on your blog or Facebook page.

An e-newsletter costs less to deliver than its direct mail counterpart, as mentioned in chapter 3, but not all clients or industries use online newsletters as the main method of contact.

As mentioned, getting subscribers to return to your website is the main reason for publishing an e-newsletter. But there's more. An e-newsletter:

- Announces new website areas that subscribers may not know exist. Site visitors sometimes fail to see new features, even if the news is posted on the home page or a "what's new" page. An e-newsletter is another avenue to tell readers what they may not recognize.
- Lets you interact with subscribers, asking them for opinions and other feedback. Announcing a survey (see chapter 3) is one way to compile their comments, providing you with immediate responses on a pending idea.
- Gives you a method to increase online sales. Most e-newsletter publishers include one offer or news about an upcoming event. The publication is being sent to people who have subscribed willingly. Why not market your goods to target candidates?
- Creates a blog and/or social media following. Subscribers may not visit your blog or social media account as often as you wish. An e-newsletter keeps them up to date on what's happening in other places where followers gather.
- Encourages readers to subscribe to a complementary print newsletter. If you publish a newsletter sent by direct mail that provides information not featured on your website or expands on the e-newsletter's topics, the online newsletter is the perfect place to drum up print version sales.

Content Development and Other Concerns

- How well do you know your clients? The more you understand their preferences, the more successful you'll be at reaching them through your publication. Even if you've taken time to query clients, it can still take months to refine your e-newsletter, its format, and frequency. The sooner you begin to lay a foundation, the quicker it will become part of your marketing campaign.
- Will the e-newsletter be published in long or short format? Many publishers start with longer formats that mirror newspapers and magazines. If

your e-newsletter's internal statistics show that readers open it consistently, you'll know that the longer version is working. If open rates are low, try a shorter version. Reduce the text by including only the first few sentences or paragraphs of an article; use a link to take readers to the rest of the story on your site. The last line of your articles might offer a product or service in conjunction with the subject.

- Are graphics an attention grabber, or is plain text best? The answer depends on many factors. Some e-newsletter readers are thrilled by visuals. It inspires them to quickly open the link. In few cases, your e-newsletter host may not allow you to add graphics. Another consideration is the rate at which e-mail hosts bar graphic-based publications from being delivered to in-boxes. E-mail hosts sometimes screen text-only e-newsletters, but because mail with graphics tends to bloat the e-mail's size, it is often treated as spam unless the subscriber adds your e-newsletter's name to their approved sender's list. You can encourage this action on your subscription page.

- If graphics are important, but you do not or cannot add them to your e-mail newsletter, a link within the publication can lead readers to a graphic version on your website, which you create without help from the e-newsletter host. You may wonder why the on-site newsletter is not considered as the main publication rather than using an e-newsletter host. The answer is simple. You're trying to bring visitors to your site. The best way to do this is through e-mail contact. The e-mail version leads visitors to your website, which increases readership and sales.

- Articles, tips, and ideas are what fill an e-newsletter, but where will you find this content if you're not an expert writer? Help lies in free article sites on the web. Writers make articles on thousands of topics available online for use in your e-newsletter, on your website, and on your blog. The article must be used as written, which includes the writer's information box at the end. This is one source of content; there are others, such as questions that clients ask accompanied by your responses. Tips that you share in video format are still another. Clients perceive anything you write as more credible than someone else's copy-and-paste article. Including your own content rather than using articles belonging to nonindustry participants elevates your status as a business, within the industry, or as a consumer ally. Also, be sure to review competitors' e-newsletters for ideas on where to find relevant content.

- How frequently will you publish the newsletter? A weekly publication is the standard for solo business owners who want to keep their business name on the minds of each subscriber. You can publish monthly if you wish or if you are just getting started and don't have enough material for a weekly publication. However, begin publishing your e-newsletter each week as quickly as possible to connect with readers who value your message and will soon purchase what you offer.

Delivery and Costs

Once you decide on the publication's contents and frequency, it's time to find a host with templates and delivery tools. Search engines will help to uncover many e-newsletter hosts. Look for them using the term "e-mail marketing software." Another technique is to look at the bottom of e-newsletters you admire. The host's logo is often found at the bottom. The logo is usually clickable, leading you straight to the host's home page for more investigation. If there is no logo, the unsubscribe link's text includes the name of the host within the URL.

Most e-newsletter hosts let you try their services free of charge for one month. This lets you test the creation and delivery controls before committing to a long-term relationship. This is a good feature. Fees for producing an e-newsletter are vastly different, depending on the host. One company may charge $100 for a year's service, while another charges $25 or more per month. There are many considerations when making your selection, including:

- Is there a wide range of templates from which to choose?
- Is the creation process easy?
- Can you include graphics?
- How many e-newsletters can you send for the monthly or yearly fee?
- Does the host provide you with the code that creates an online subscription box?
- How easy is it for you to import e-mail addresses collected elsewhere into the host's system?
- How responsive is the host to your questions? (To test this, send at least two questions via e-mail during the trial process.)
- How extensive are each host's statistics, and which numbers do you really need?

You will pay the host to provide you with templates and means for delivery, but in most cases you will not charge your subscribers to receive the news. This is the cost of marketing that we home-based and solo business owners pay. Treat the fees associated with publishing an online newsletter as an investment in your business rather than an expense. E-newsletters allow you to tell clients about products and services as well as act as a partner in their business or personal lives. Most of all, your e-newsletter must lead readers back to your website, blog, or social media account as much as possible. That will ensure its overall success.

Don't be dismayed if your e-newsletter isn't distributed to thousands of subscribers. It's better to deliver to a few hundred buyers and referrals than thousands of browsers. Once my e-newsletter reaches the 1,000 subscribers range, I start purging the mailing list, unsubscribing anyone who has not opened my publication in three months. Delivery to each person costs money. I have the right to determine who receives my news. So do you.

Marketing Strategies

Making clients and prospects aware of your e-news can be accomplished on and off the web. Here are five methods:

1. Use the HTML code provided by the host company to create an online subscription box. This template is to be pasted on most, if not all, of your website, blog pages, and through a Facebook application. Many sites contain a header template that duplicates anything within the header region on every page. That will let you paste the subscription box once for duplication on each site or blog page. Try this procedure during the free trial subscription.
2. Create a dedicated subscription page on your website. This page will inform visitors about your newsletter's contents and provide the subscription box.

> **Sample subscription page:** www.giftbasketbusiness.com/newsletter.htm

3. Notify clients by postcard. Starting an online newsletter gives you another reason to contact customers by direct mail. Postcards are also sent to anyone who's shown interest in the past.

4. Include notice about the e-newsletter in your e-mail signature. Each time you send an e-mail, it will include a link to your subscription page.

5. Inform everyone about the newsletter on your business card, stationery, brochures, and other print literature.

Create a long-term vision for your e-newsletter before you begin. Publish your news for at least a year. Then decide how to continue with new material and updates to past topics. Also, use surveys to learn how the publication can best serve its readers. This feedback will elevate your motivation.

Creating an Online Press Room

An online press room, also known as a media room, is mandatory on your site. This virtual media kit works to market your business and industry expertise. The press room can be one or more pages, depending on the amount of information you share and how the data are distributed. It also depends on your industry longevity. The longer you've been in business, the more expertise you'll post online. Here's an example of how to structure an online press room.

Index. This first page introduces the reader to the site and provides a breakdown of what's included on subsequent pages.

Backgrounder. The second page is a synopsis of your business and your experience —who you are, how and when the business began, milestones, and affiliated associations.

Press relations. The third page lets readers know which media—newspapers, magazines, television, radio, cable, and satellite—hosted your appearances and printed your expert quotes. Separate the details by media type. If links are available to online interviews, this is where you add links to those stories. A sample of this media room page is found at the end of the chapter.

Industry facts and figures. Share expertise about your industry by providing insights and statistics. Citings can be collected from your own surveys and from industry associations with access to statistics. Be sure to properly attribute outside sources.

Frequently asked questions. A list of ten to twelve questions and answers elevates your expertise. General questions, rather than technical, are best in this section. The information you provide here encourages the media to call for expert solutions and prospects to call for consultative projects. See a sample media room at www.giftbasketbusiness.com/contact.htm.

Books, DVDs, catalogs. List the products that support your expertise. If you've written a book, whether self-published or through a traditional publisher, scan the cover and add it to the media room. Place the book's synopsis below the scanned cover. Customer comments about the book add relevance. Look for these comments in mailed correspondence, e-mailed notes, and online bookstores' comments sections if your book is sold through these sites.

The bottom of each media section page includes information on how to contact you. See how this is done in the sample media room page.

Photographs and videos complement the press room content, so if you have photos or videos that show interaction with customers or industry professionals, add those pictures on these pages. That will help to create an informative section visited by media, customers, and competitors.

Getting up-close and personal with media broadcasters taps into a powerful outlet that markets your message to a local, national, or international audience. Secure a publicist's help or pursue this marketing avenue on your own. Each broadcast segment has the potential to create a lifetime of sales.

We've covered a lot of ground in this chapter. Establishing your website or blog takes many steps. Rest assured—you have the ability to complete each step. No marketing plan can move forward without an Internet presence. List your goals, complete the objectives, launch your site or blog, set up your e-newsletter, create an online press room, and begin reaping the rewards that occur when the web becomes part of your business strategy.

Sample Online Media Room Page

CLIENT LIST, NEWS COVERAGE, SEMINAR LOCATIONS

OUR CLIENTS
Barnes & Noble
Macy's
Main Cards & Gifts
MetLife

NEWS COVERAGE
National Newspapers
Chicago Tribune
Los Angeles Times
New York Newsday
Orange County Register
New York Times
Washington Post

CLIENT LIST, NEWS COVERAGE, SEMINAR LOCATIONS

National Magazines

Black Enterprise

Costco Connection

Entrepreneur

Forbes

Inc. Magazine

Television appearances

ABC-TV

Bloomberg News

CNBC

CNN

Fox Channel 5 (NY)

Seminar locations

Atlanta

Boston

Chicago

Dallas

Denver

Los Angeles

Miami

New York

Washington, DC

Trade Magazines

Fancy Food

Florists' Review

Flowers&

Gifts & Decorative Accessories

Gourmet News

Contact Us

Comments

Share your opinion about this site on our comments page.

Partnerships

E-mail questions about business matters to Mike Hanna at mhanna@mysite.com.

Press

We are always happy to speak with the media. E-mail your questions to Henry Hudson, media manager, at hhudson@mysite.com, or call (555) 893-1600 for fast response.

Our Location

Solo Marketing Book

PO Box 91

Paramus, NJ 07653

Voice (973) 279-2799

Security Issues and Solutions

If you've just started a business, you may be surprised to realize how important security is in relation to marketing. Here's the connection: If you don't protect your property, whether online content or physical products, you will have little or nothing to market. This chapter looks at three types of small-business security issues: physical property, intellectual property, and computer data. We'll discuss copyrights, patents, trademarks, computer back-up systems, and other protection tools.

Perhaps you've never considered securing your products or intellectual property, or maybe you thought there was no available protection. Everything can be covered with some measure of security. It doesn't mean that someone won't duplicate your work, but it will slow them down or make a project too difficult to copy.

Security Problems from the Trenches

Marketing keeps you behind a desk, creating letters and brochures that offer and close deals. It also takes you out into the world to mingle with people who want to know more about your business and how it benefits them. Some of us cherish the interaction, while others shudder at the thought of leaving their offices to meet the public.

The truth of the matter is, business owners who want to be successful must occasionally leave the confines of their offices. Good businesspeople all seem to have one thing in common: They're keenly aware of the difference between people looking to buy and people looking to copy. Prospects look at the merchandise. You can almost see the wheels turning in their heads as they recognize how buying the item makes a tedious chore easier or a rough surface smoother. The copiers view an item with a completely different focus.

Buying is not on this person's mind. He's wondering, "How can I copy this and make money from it?" You may have seen this expression, and perhaps the same has panned across your face in the past. We cannot stop anyone from duplicating our style and making minor changes, but we are able to create and implement security systems to protect materials that have taken years to perfect.

My sister, Cassandra, is an example of a security-conscious entrepreneur. She's in the cutthroat world of crafts. People who make items from scratch often develop ideas from what they see in magazines and craft show booths. Cassandra answers questions from potential customers cautiously. Some booth visitors admit that they're also into crafts and proceed to ask proprietary questions. She won't respond, which forces some visitors to exit in search of another, less security-conscious crafter.

I was born with a trusting heart and flair for sharing the most-precise details. It has been beneficial in the teaching arena but a weakness elsewhere. After books, CDs, and booklets were lifted several times from my own display tables, I finally learned how to secure my products, even when my back is turned.

We home-based and solo business owners market great ideas and products every day. Those same ideas and products need a built-in security system. Here are some examples.

Online

Photographs. Artists sell by displaying images of their work on the web. They know that watermarks added on top of portraits and paintings decrease the chance of having the work lifted and posted elsewhere. A watermark can be removed, but it takes time and energy. Thieves pass over protected works in search of easier targets.

Articles and reports. Website owners who educate visitors on everything from baby care to senior services make data available in article, report, video, audio, and tip formats. Some material is general knowledge. Other data provide advice. Then there's intellectual material that is so coveted that it's only posted in membership sites in a format that discourages duplication. This type of material includes statistics and industry data (upcoming trends on fashion, color, etc.).

Offline

Publications. Renting a booth at a trade or consumer show may be part of your marketing strategy. However, your blood may boil if you watch a person at your booth standing motionless, reading a sample of a for-sale report cover to cover, only to put it down and walk away. This is why some of us do not exhibit at shows unless we can provide sample materials through a computer slideshow or invest in mock-up publications that display a portion of the text.

Technological data. It's difficult to protect all of your products while traveling alone. You bring products to sell at a particular event, and for the most part, everyone abides by the honor system of taking only what they plan to buy. But sometimes things get out of control, and you may be missing items that were not paid for, especially CDs, DVDs, and other compact materials.

Physical Security

Home-based business owners who sell expensive products learn how to protect them while traveling to demonstrations and consumer shows. They use bars, locks, and cables that clamp onto surfaces. These supplies provide temporary security without damaging furniture. Even with this type of protection, these owners can share stories on how security was cut, stripped, or swiped along with the product.

Security isn't just a problem for expensive items. It's also necessary for anything you don't want to lose, no matter what the cost. As an example, your favorite pen is attached to a thin cord that stays around your neck. The pen emerges from its compartment when needed, but somehow it disappears. You look down at the cord to see a penless cap. Your own security has been breached. It's an unfortunate circumstance that may be small to some, but it's not to the person whose pen is missing.

Let's look at two more security issues.

Trade Show Dilemmas

I've attended trade shows for more than twenty-two years and have seen evidence of careless security in practically every aisle. The New York Incentive Rewards & Recognition Expo and the Motivation Show, two wonderful events that every marketer needs to attend (more on these shows in chapter 9), is where you can take free marketing samples from most booths. Personalized rubber bands, eye makeup remover, lotions, gift cards, chocolates, and logo-customized pens are some of the treasured items. I've seen attendees sweep their arms across a table in an attempt to deposit everything into their show bags. That's the type of security breach that occurs if an exhibitor isn't watching.

Solution: Qualify each recipient to receive a sample product. This tactic works for exhibitors with a limited number of samples. I've seen this process for distributing gift cards, desk calendars, and plush items. Long lines form with attendees waiting their turn to speak with a representative and receive the coveted gift, if they qualify. Not all exhibitors go this route. Some have thousands of samples to distribute. Scattering items across a table to create a frenzy of excitement while fielding questions from inquisitive attendees works for them.

Another solution is to use empty containers or covers as visual stimulus. These let customers see what you're selling without having the real products on the table. Bring additional containers to replace any that disappear. This is an option for Roger Green as he begins creating DVDs and similar media. It's how I protect materials when displaying products at a show.

Positioning Problems

As a home-based business owner, I travel by myself, but that doesn't mean I'm always alone. I have colleagues in California who accompany me to events where I speak about small business topics. The setting can be a small hotel meeting room or a cavernous convention hall. My friends provide top-notch security in places where I cannot control what happens at the buying table. One colleague followed a potential buyer as she drifted into a faraway corner with a book she hadn't yet purchased. Were the book's words so mesmerizing that she could not account for her actions? My friend retrieved the book which was, unfortunately, not purchased after the detailed inspection.

A different event resulted in a loss. Another colleague temporarily vacated a sales table to complete an order with a customer seated in front of the room. Books for sale and other items were positioned on the inside of the entry door. On the other side was a walkway used by hundreds of show attendees walking to other destinations. Two people walked in, grabbed books, and walked out. My friend was approaching the table when this occurred, and she chose not to raise her voice because of my ongoing presentation. She made the right decision but was upset because of the theft. Still, I could not have sold as much product on that day without her help.

Solution: Prepare a sales form listing all items available at your event and staple it to the back of your presentation materials for distribution to each attendee. Add payment details (cash only, credit cards, etc.) and your website address as information for those who take the sheet but aren't ready to order. If a person considers making a purchase, the form will allow you to expedite the process without vacating the sales table. Providing customer service is one thing, but leaving the goods unmanned to focus on one customer is dangerous.

Creating a sales form takes little time, especially if you have a form on your website. Copy and paste it into a word processing document. Then make changes as needed and save the form for future events.

Let anyone who is ready to buy at a seminar do so at the table rather than from another location. It's impossible to secure multiple areas when you're one person, so don't try.

Intellectual Security: Paranoia Is Healthy

It's perfectly normal to be fearful about your work and other intellectual property being taken and used in a manner you did not approve. Such fear moves you to action. What type of registration is available? How can you guard against theft? Where are the tools, and are they affordable? These thoughts and many others run through your mind. There are methods that calm those fears, even if security is not available for everything.

You may have heard that ideas cannot be protected. That is true. The US Patent and Trademark Office (USPTO) states that "a trademark is a word, phrase, symbol or design, or a combination thereof, that identifies and distinguishes the source of the goods of one party from those of others." The same is true if you plan to apply for a copyright. The US Copyright Office states that "a copyright is a form of protection grounded in the US Constitution and granted by law for original works of authorship fixed in a tangible medium of expression. Copyright covers both published and unpublished works." This law applies to the above formats, but it does not apply to an idea.

Here's one of the key points, from the Copyright Office website, on what cannot be protected: "Copyright does not protect facts, ideas, systems, or methods of operation, although it may protect the way these things are expressed." Still, there are many weapons within your reach to provide security in a broad sense.

United States Patent and Trademark Office: www.uspto.gov
United States Copyright Office: www.copyright.gov

Be aware that not everything needs security or is a candidate for the same type of protection. Janet Ross, the CPA in chapter 1, doesn't need to copyright the articles in her marketing brochures because she didn't write the content, and the entire product is made for her by an outsourcing firm. She does, however, need to protect her clients' accounting information. Hard copies of tax statements require storage in a waterproof safe secured by a combination lock. Statements housed within her computer are accessed by a security code, and a backup set of clients' files were either copied onto an external computer hard drive within her office or stored through a subscription-based online backup system. If her computer files become corrupted, the external drive and online system provide methods for instant retrieval. Janet has also learned that some colleagues store clients' records on CD on a yearly basis, which is placed in a separate area from the waterproof safe files. Janet plans to do the same.

Roger Green, chapter 1's golf specialist, has no need to patent the golf clubs and supplies he sells. That's covered by the products' manufacturers. He does plan to trademark his business name, Teed Up. Roger will also create a program to help other golf specialists start youth golf schools in other states. He believes the blueprint he's developed of working with school officials and parents will serve as a model that other areas can follow. A text manual and set of tutorial DVDs and CDs to teach and train golf to youth and adults is also part of Roger's plan. When completed, the materials qualify as intellectual property securable through copyright.

These are examples of how home-based business owners take action to provide security to products and services they develop or maintain.

Advice for Non-US Residents

If you reside outside of the US, the US Patent and Trademark Division and the US Copyright Office can assist you with some of your protection requirements. Visit their websites for more information.

The following Product Creation Chart lists materials you may be developing or already have available and their corresponding types of protection. If you don't see items specific to your business, the respective websites for patents, trademarks, and copyrights will steer you in the right direction.

Product Creation Chart

Product or Service	Types of Protection			
	Copyright	Patent	Trademark	No Protection
Books, booklets, brochures, articles, and anything in written form	X			
CDs, DVDs, anything in audio/visual format	X			
Business name, product name			X	
Model or design element		X		
Music	X			
Architectural or similar drawings	X			
Choreographic work	X			
Inventions		X		
Symbols for identification			X	
Ideas, methods, systems, concepts				X

Quick Copyright Tips

Copyright protects most printed material. Once you've written a song, article, or training system, it's your property and is copyrighted even if you choose not to pay for copyright protection. You may have heard of friends who practice their own type of security against claims, people who mail the materials to themselves and don't open it as a form of protection. At trade shows I've heard many attorneys who specialize in copyright law say that this practice isn't necessary. When a pen connects with any type of writing surface to form written content or words are typed and saved within a computer software program, the result is automatically your copyrighted material, unless the words are already someone else's property. (For example, the slogan "just do it" belongs to Nike, so don't try to claim it as part of your business name.) In fact, the Copyright Office's frequently asked questions section states that "your work is under copyright protection the moment it is created and fixed in a tangible form that is perceptible either directly or with the aid of a machine or device." Obtain the services of an attorney versed in this topic if you require guidance.

If the time comes to sue another party for illegal use of your material, a certificate of copyright issued by the US Copyright Office provides you with a stronger case. You'll be able to prove what is yours and when it was copyrighted. That's the advantage over not registering your property, even though you can still go to court with uncopyrighted material to argue your case.

Visit the US Copyright Office online and print out the correct form for the material you wish to protect. Forms can also be requested by mail or found and copied at local libraries. As of this book's publication, the copyright fee is $35 for online filing and $65 for by-mail filing, which is a bargain to protect your intellectual property. Forms are available to register different types of literary works. Each form is self-explanatory. If you neglect to complete part of the submission, the Copyright Office will contact you for clarification.

One or two copies of the material must accompany your by-mail submission and payment. The number of required copies depends on whether the content is published or unpublished. It is recommended that you copyright completed work as soon as possible. It can take up to five months to receive your copyright certificate; however, your work is still protected during that time.

Trademarks—Then and Now

Some business owners protect their company names and logos with a registered trademark. They see the trademark as a long-term investment. They know that their business will be a viable and profitable operation, not a hobby. It can still take a while to start the trademark process, but when it's time, the owner moves forward to complete the work and place an ® symbol after the company name.

That's what I did years after starting my business. Things weren't the way they are now. Today USPTO online lets you research names from your home or office computer. In the early 1990s I had to drive ten miles to a metropolitan library that housed two computers for researching business names and symbols and a stack of disks that divided the trademark information by last letter.

No one had registered my business name, so I copied the forms and submitted my trademark claim. A USPTO attorney contacted me by mail. He explained minor edits to be made and the deadline for resubmission. I went through this process twice for the trademark because I didn't understand what to do the first time. A few months later an official notice arrived by mail stating that the trademark was official.

Solo business owners secure their company names and symbols so that no one else can use that particular name or symbol for other products or services. Your registered trademark gives you the right to have an attorney send a cease-and-desist letter to anyone using the same words or symbol. My attorney did this for me when I showed her proof of another party using my business name. The other party's attorney formally replied that the name would no longer be used by his client.

Trademark protection outside of the United States is available, but the cease-and-desist process may have a few more hurdles than same-country rules. Your attorney can explain the details if a problem develops. The USPTO website also provides information on worldwide trademark protection.

The USPTO, like the Copyright Office, is adept at explaining all trademark facts through a frequently asked questions section. You will learn what can and cannot be trademarked, the difference between the TM and registered ® symbols, and more. You can also print registration forms to secure your business name, slogan, and brand symbol by mail, or you can submit your application online.

Trademark protection forms are more difficult to complete than copyright forms, but business owners just like you perform this task every day. Attorneys that specialize in this work are available to oversee the entire process if you have more money than time or believe that an attorney will streamline the work for you.

The current trademark application fee starts at $275. If you plan to submit a trademark request, do so with diligence. The fee is not refundable if you decide not to pursue the trademark after submitting the paperwork.

Patent Protection

Invention property rights, design manufacturing and improvements, and new plant production processes are the main focus of patents. Patents are the only form of intellectual protection for which drawings, usually assigned to copyright protection, are entered to explain the invention's details. When filing, the patent office makes this procedure easy by encouraging online submissions.

> **United States Patent and Trademark Office:** www.uspto.gov/patents/process/index.jsp

You have choices when filing a patent:

1. Submit the application on your own.
2. Contract an attorney who is versed in patent submission.
3. Use a legitimate patent submission firm.

It is advised that you check and double-check an attorney's or submission firm's credentials before trusting them with the property rights information you've worked so hard to create. Some firms are legitimate, and some are not. Trusted sources who have successfully submitted a patent with third-party assistance may be willing to recommend reputable help.

Strategies to Protect Your Property

Now that you have a general idea of how marketing and security are linked, let's get into specifics that secure your property.

CDs, DVDs, and Similar Technology

We solo business owners who travel alone throughout the world to sell our products find the experience to be rewarding, exciting, and tiring all at once. On one end, you must prepare information about your services and create products for sale at the event. On the other end, you must be a gracious host when speaking to potential customers and a stern security officer as you make sure that items don't disappear from sight.

Some tabled items must be the exact product that a customer will receive by mail or other means. Others can be replicas or imitations. The more objects that can pose as the real thing, the better for your security and peace of mind. CDs, DVDs, and similar media are the easiest items to imitate. They are valuable property that disappears quickest from a table or display, so you must show replicas. Then you hand customers the real item once the purchase is made.

Here is how to create CD and DVD imitations:

1. Collect disks that contain no important data. This includes free trial disks from other companies and disks distributed free of charge at retail and postal outlets. Do not use blank CDs that you've purchased. That wastes your money and depletes a costly product.
2. Create labels similar to the ones placed on your genuine audio/visual products. If these labels are not made in your office, ask the label supplier to provide you with extras. Place the labels onto the replicas.
3. Place the imitation disks into jewel cases to simulate what clients will receive when making a purchase. This step is not mandatory, but do so if you believe that type of presentation encourages sales.

4. Apply a price sticker directly on the label. It will identify the disk as an imitation so you don't sell it unintentionally.

5. Write an "S" on the label using a marker color that's easy to detect. The letter "S" identifies the disk as a sample. Use another letter if preferred. This label marking serves as double protection against selling the product in case the price sticker is removed.

Storage boxes that house DVDs need not be filled with media. Simply insert a label into the storage box's outer transparent cover. Mark and sticker it in the same format as CDs.

No one needs to touch the real product until a sale is under way or complete. Products containing genuine data are kept under or behind the table, out of customers' hands. Still, be careful of how you handle the real thing. Some prospects are brazen, walking behind your table or display to rifle through the box of genuine goods when your attention is turned elsewhere. Such actions show that security will always be an issue no matter what controls are put into place.

My products are displayed on a side table that attendees view before and after my seminars. At the end of my talks, I announce that items for sale can be viewed on the table, but purchases must be made through me. Many people purchase, and others have questions. Fifteen minutes after one of my presentations ended, the room was empty, and so was the table. Every imitation CD and DVD was gone. If any had been genuine media, I would have been annoyed at myself for leaving products unattended. The genuine CDs and DVDs were under the main table in front of me. The table media were sample software disks received by mail. I began to wonder if my closing remarks encouraged attendees to take the tabled items, but I recalled being very specific about buying directly through me. This security system has helped me to market without the stress of manning a table while speaking with people who hear my presentation.

Security is needed for nonspeakers as well. For example, you may host a table display at a chamber of commerce event or another gathering on land or sea. A conversation can become so intense that you suddenly lose track of table products. No matter what setting or types of people attend, there are times when items will disappear. Even if products clearly state "do not take," things somehow get lost. But the problem is lessened by displaying imitations rather than genuine goods.

Protecting valuable media is easy. Create replicas to show customers what's available, and then present genuine products when they're ready to buy. Now you can display and sell in comfort.

Books, Booklets, and Other Matter

Everyone wants to read parts of a book before they buy or don't buy it. That's what's so great about the few bookstores that still exist today. They let browsers read everything in the store, curl the pages, spill coffee and crumbs within publications, photograph pages with a tablet or camera, and then leave the store without a single purchase. But you're not a bookstore. You create publications that fit within a certain niche category, so what you sell is information that can't be found anywhere else. This fact allows you to keep some, if not all, of your materials under wraps before it is sold. It may seem difficult to do, and it's obviously difficult for browsers to comprehend. The way in which browsers seem to read all the text within your publications and then quiz you on the contents before walking away empty handed is a major reason why home-based and solo business owners rarely display their products in the open. They'd rather sell such items from the comfort of their offices, through their websites, or through an online affiliate. However, there are times when events lend themselves to additional sales, so security precautions are needed to show printed matter without letting everyone use your display as a library or bookstore.

> **What is an affiliate?:** http://bit.ly/m1S1m

What about customers who buy your material and return it after obvious signs of duplication? Not all customers do this, but it does happen. There's no law that says you, as a company that produces unique information, must carry a full refund policy. In other words, your policy can state one of the following:

- No returns
- No returns after fifteen days
- Restocking charge of (percentage) for all returns

Many customer service experts say that the more liberal the return policy, the more apt customers will be to buy. However, not all businesses can follow these rules, especially if what you sell is unique to the marketplace. Look at the return policies of other industry participants. Do they offer full refunds? If so, take a closer look at what they sell. Is it similar to your products? Be sure to compare your findings on a balanced ratio. For example, it's customary for a major bookstore to offer customers full refunds. If you sell your own books within a company that does not function as a bookstore, you do not have to offer customers a full refund.

One of my companies does not allow returns because the printed materials, DVDs, and other products are so specialized that refunds are not an option. My catalogs and websites explain, very specifically, what is contained in each product so that customers can make wise choices. Customers are encouraged to call the office for additional information and to place their order by phone instead of in the online store. My no-return policy is the front-runner for the entire industry it represents. Other industry sellers have also decided not to allow returns. Be sure that your terms are clearly stated on the order form, in your online store, and anywhere else that customers view and order your products.

You may think that a no-return policy works against sales, but that's not true. The policy will serve to deter customers who frequently return products from ordering in the first place.

In addition, you'll have fewer return and adjustment problems.

Books

It's impossible to display a partial self-published or traditionally-published book, so do the next best thing: Make a maximum of three books available for browsers to review. These books are samples that cannot be sold because they are bruised or somewhat damaged. Rather than throw them away, such books are useful to sell the good stock. If someone wants to see a book and all three are in browsers' hands, announce to all that others are waiting to view the samples and that you also have books available for immediate purchase.

Another option is to sell the book on-site but not bring it with you. One-person businesses with more than books for sale often bring only the products that have the highest margin for revenue. Traditionally-published books seldom fit that category. For example, if DVDs cost $5 wholesale and sell for $30 retail, the margin is $25. If a book cost $10 wholesale and $20 retail, the margin is lower ($10). In addition, books are heavier to carry or ship and take up more space under the sales table. This is why some business owners leave books at the office, opting to bring one sample and collect orders on-site. Offering a buying incentive such as free shipping or a free gift with purchase is a method to boost sales of items not at the event.

Booklets and Custom Publications

It takes many hours to craft materials uniquely specific to one industry. Event visitors understand this and know a specialty publication when they see one. The item is taken from the table, absorbed from beginning to end, and then placed back on the table without a sale. Instead of a display acting as a sales table, it acts as a library. I've seen this many times, and it happened to me until I learned how to secure my property before the sale.

The way to protect your booklets, wire-bound documents, and other unique materials is by enclosing them in clear, flat plastic sleeves or bags. The sleeves are fused on three ends and open at the top. Insert each publication in a sleeve, fold the top downward to the back, and add tape or a sticker to keep the sleeve closed until purchased. This, along with keeping the publications behind the counter with DVDs and other media, is a good way to stop browsers from opening and reading items for sale.

There's a method for displaying booklets as your for-sale material outside of sharing the entire contents. Let an empty cover or title page act as a sample. The publication's table of contents is displayed alongside the cover, which familiarizes browsers with the information in each booklet. Browsers may ask why the actual booklet isn't available for viewing. Responses such as, "This setup makes it easier for you to make the right buying choices," or "I want to make sure there is enough material for everyone to buy," are appropriate, as they express a concern for customer service and accommodation.

Backup Options in the Office

You spent the week creating books, teleseminars, and other marketing materials. The weekend arrives, and you carefully shut down the computer as you do every Friday. On Monday morning you start your day by pressing the computer button. Nothing happens. Plugs are checked to ensure connections. You even unplug the hard drive from the surge protector and replug it. Still nothing. Your computer is dead. Even if you had renewed your computer's service contract, there's no telling whether your data will be intact if you can get the machine up and running. Now you're really in a panic. What's the next step?

This scene occurs every day in offices around the world. Large corporations suffer when a computer terminal suddenly does not work. They have a dedicated information technology (IT) department to call for assistance, while you are probably your own IT manager. Computer security is mandatory to protect trade secrets and intellectual property from people who want to take shortcuts, but it's even more critical to protect us from our own negligence. How many times have you said to yourself, "I'm going to get a backup system," and it's never done? The cost of installing backup security to a computer system amounts to pennies compared to the aggravation and time it will take to re-create letters, audios, forms, and plans, not to mention any data provided to you by clients. What will clients think of you when you tell them about the lost data? They may not have another copy. That's just a sample of what happens when computer security is neglected.

> Data loss not only lowers your daily productivity, it can also end business, permanently. That's the chance taken each day when you work without a computer backup system.

Computer Security Strategies

Admittedly, it's difficult to wade through computer security options and choose backup equipment, but remember: Lost data will end your solo enterprise. The following tutorial will make the process smoother. First, choose the statement that fits your business lifestyle. Then read the situation that matches.

Problem: I need backup for my office computer, something small enough to keep out of sight and that can be transported if needed.

Solution: An external hard drive.

Problem: I need backup for the office computer, but I also need to access files on the road. Some files contain too much data to load onto my laptop.

Solution: Internet computer storage, cloud storage, or a large-capacity flash drive.

Problem: I work in a space so tight that an extra piece of equipment will cramp me. But I still need to backup certain files.

Solution: Cloud storage or similar type of online backup software.

External Hard Drive

My first computer backup system was equipment that attached to my computer's parallel port. The product stored the data on 250 megabyte disks. Today, my healthy paranoia insists that I back up my computer with both online and external hard drive equipment.

The words "external hard drive" refer to the ability to store massive amounts of computer data on a storage system that resides outside of a traditional desktop or laptop computer. Every computer maintains an internal storage unit loaded with software that tells the computer what to do when it starts up and dispenses other instructions depending on commands transmitted by keyboard or mouse. An external hard drive acts as a second computer brain, storing every file or specific files you wish to save in case the internal drive fails to work. An external hard drive plugs into any computer or laptop for easy access to the stored data. It's easy to install by simply plugging the external equipment into your computer's USB port and placing the product's disk into the computer's CD drive. From there, follow the installation guide, and you can start backing up all files, folders, and media immediately and create a backup schedule for daily (recommended) or monthly security.

You've moved from working with no security to installing a system that will become habitual every day. Think about all the man-hours you'll save retrieving your work if anything happens to your computer, and the investment is worth the few minutes of installation.

Internet Computer Storage and Access

What if a fire occurred in your office, destroying both your computer and external hard drive? All data would be gone, with no chance of recovery. An alternative to having an external hard drive in your office is to back up your data using an Internet-based backup system. There are companies that secure your data and give you access to the same data outside of the office.

Add to this the fact that everyone based in a home office doesn't solely work at home. Many of us travel thousands of miles each year. Having access to client information while on the road is usually easy, because the client already has all files in his office. If you need access to your own work while traveling, that can pose a problem, especially if you neglect to bring the external hard drive or files on a flash drive. Additionally, laptop computers and tablets are often targeted by thieves who watch your every move. You can take steps to be one jump ahead of criminals, but a single misstep or distraction may separate you from your computer. The situation is worse if the laptop contains sensitive information. That's why many solo owners don't load financial and other secretive data onto their laptops. Instead, they use Internet options that give them access to critical data.

Cloud storage: http://bit.ly/W3DWkJ

Online Data and Cloud Storage

Internet-based data storage firms (including cloud storage) specialize in backing up your computer files onto their servers, transferring all files or the files of your choosing safely and securely until you change the contents or retrieve the data from anywhere in the world.

Does the thought of placing your most valuable content onto another company's servers make you nervous? You're not alone, but thousands of solo, small, and large companies use these services every day. Firms that protect your data make sure they're safe from attack and are convenient to access by:

1. Backing up your data on multiple servers in case one incurs problems.
2. Scanning every file added to their servers for viruses and other data-eating worms.
3. Encrypting your content so that no one can read the data except you.

Most services let you back up data daily or on a pre-set schedule. Many offer back-ups on a free trial basis before you invest in the service. After that there is a fee, but it is affordable and paid monthly or yearly. These data security firms make storage easy by offering one-click services to back up your material.

USB Flash Drive

Did you ever think that your most-prized files could dangle at the end of a lanyard worn around your neck? That's the beauty of today's technology. External drives known as flash drives are light enough to carry by hand in a backpack or briefcase, and office computers are accessible after downloading software to keep you con-nected to files wherever you travel. Flash drives act as a feather-light storage option and make lack of security inexcusable.

The flash drive has become an indispensable piece of equipment. Its small size, convenience, and ability to store large files allow certain data to stay secure while traveling. This product is shorter than the average pen and conveniently transfers data between computers or protects files in and out of the office.

Flash drive definition: http://bit.ly/TSzlDq

The average flash drive storage size is between 1 to 2 gigabytes. Every office supply store, warehouse club, and electronics retailer sells them, often at sale prices. Product prices steadily decrease as newer flash drives with more storage space become available. Flash drives can be customized with your name and logo to serve as marketing tools.

All computers contain USB ports. A flash drive plugs into a USB port to transfer data from a computer to the flash drive and vice versa. Using a flash drive is much easier than attempting to network two computers just to send one or two files to the other.

As we've seen, marketing and security work together to keep your business protected against intrusions and interruptions, whether by mistake or on purpose. Marketing cannot function properly without a full serving of security. Make sure that both parts are monitored and updated to maximize productivity.

Gifts and Other Incentives

Now that you've learned how marketing and security complement each other, perhaps the concept of gifts, incentives, and marketing won't be a big stretch to your imagination. Marketing activities motivate clients to buy from you and to recommend your products and services to their personal and business associates. Marketing is also based on the steps you take to develop and manage relationships with clients and others in the marketing pipeline. The process is similar to tending a garden. You till the land, buy and plant seeds, water and nurture the space, and weed and talk to it occasionally. In the end you hope to build a beautiful patch where one didn't exist in the past. This chapter focuses on gift giving to strengthen business relationships.

Gifts and other incentives work to secure loyalty and trust. Many companies, including your competitors, do little to create allegiance. They collect money, say "thanks," and either end the relationship or place it in the dormant stage. The negligence is the same online. No card, no reminders, no follow-up whatsoever. No wonder buyers go to other sources when it's time to purchase again.

Your strategy will be different from all others. Prospects who subscribe to your e-newsletter will receive, by e-mail, a keepsake list of the top fifty ways to benefit from what you sell. Clients who purchase from you receive handwritten notes expressing your appreciation. Customers who have invested money in your products and services receive an end-of-year gift, depending on the amount spent. Some will receive a gift card (also called a reward card), others get an edible gift, and another group receives complimentary consulting help by phone. These are examples of gifts and incentives that thrill clients, convincing them to keep buying and referring others to your brick-and-mortar or virtual door. Such items are beyond affordable and necessary—they're priceless in their ability to create business opportunities and profits every month of the year. Your plan to find and distribute gifts and incentives will make your business thrive.

How Incentives Increase Business

Sears continues to be one of my favorite stores. It may not be high on another person's list, but a Sears' salesman was the first person to send me a thank-you note for buying an appliance. It included his business card. I'm sure the note was part of the job's requirement, but those few words of appreciation started a relationship that continues today. It acted as a return incentive. There are products I'll buy only at Sears because of that note, and I continue to receive one each time I buy a new appliance.

That card was my introduction to postsales service years before I considered starting a business. Its influence led me to include a handwritten appreciation note with each order mailed to my customers, as detailed in chapter 3. At the end of my first year in business, I wanted to express my client appreciation with something that accompanied a holiday card. I searched for an item of value that wouldn't strain my budget and found a chocolate manufacturer that sold solid milk chocolate boxes. The box lid was also chocolate, and inside the box were espresso beans dipped in chocolate. My clients would appreciate the product even as they ate the entire gift. I ordered thirty boxes and wrapped the outside packaging of each with a bow.

Twenty of the clients called to rave about the gift. They were so delighted that they asked me to send the same chocolate box to many of their clients. I placed an order for 150 more, shipping them before the holiday. I could not have guessed that my appreciation gift would act as an incentive for my own customers. My quarterly sales were more profitable, and I added new clients to my roster, right in time for the New Year.

Each year a good friend who owns a retail gift shop explores new methods to clear out old merchandise. He reads gift trade magazines and attends business shows to learn how retailers worldwide get rid of slow sellers. One winning strategy lets him use the old merchandise as a sales incentive. He puts several products in small and large bags, placing the bags on a table monitored by an employee. The bags are cinched with a ribbon or staple so no one can see what's inside. Customers purchasing a specific dollar amount of store merchandise receive a bag of goodies.

Small bags are for $40 to $74 purchases, while larger bags are for $75 or more in sales. Customers who purchase less than $40 also receive one gift contained in a small pouch. The event is held at different times of the year so that customers don't know when it will occur. This incentive creates a frenzy of in-store activity, acts as a magnet for new customers to come in and shop, and clears out slow-moving products just in time to stock shelves for a new selling season.

Another friend does the same thing, but with an Internet twist. She's a retailer who publishes a highly successful online newsletter filled with gift-giving ideas that points readers to her website to see special and everyday gift assortments. There is no walk-in store, so this retailer uses her e-newsletter as an incentive. One contest instructs readers to e-mail her when they open the newsletter. The first subscriber who sends an e-mail stating that they opened the publication wins selected merchandise, which is mailed directly to their location. She receives hundreds of e-mails, all from readers who hope to be the winner. Beautiful containers, plush animals, and other new merchandise are mailed free of charge for personal use or resale within the winner's store.

Products lead the pack when it comes to incentives. I've watched television shows that reveal the enthusiasm expressed by cosmetic representatives who receive costume jewelry from their managers at monthly meetings. The jewelry may cost $5, but to a representative who's sold $500 of cosmetics, receiving another bauble is reward in itself.

Don't dismiss service-based gifts and incentives. Like the online retailer, you may need to use an out-of-the-box twist to inspire clients. Consulting services are popular and can be offered to customers whom you consider as VIPs or others just below that designation. Maps may not seem like an exciting incentive, but one that tells the history of baseball or another sport, along with the location of every ballpark in the United States, is worth gold to an enthusiast. A golf map is an item Roger Green considers giving to his golf clients. Anyone who enjoys the sport will appreciate it.

How Incentives Aid Your Plan

Do you believe that sending appreciation gifts to loyal clients will increase sales? Many companies believe that appreciation gifts work. In 2012 the Incentive Research Foundation conducted a survey, which reveals the popularity of gift giving to customers, employees, and representatives. Here's the list of products ranked most popular as consumer incentives:

1. Electronics
2. Golf items
3. Luggage
4. Housewares
5. Gift cards (non-specialty store)
6. Jewelry/watches
7. Office accessories
8. Clothing/apparel
9. Food
10. Specialty store gift cards

This list proves the popularity of general (Visa, MasterCard, etc.) and specialty store gift cards. Cards allow clients to choose the gift they want; you don't have to worry about making the wrong selection. In addition, gift cards are acceptable when you're not sure what to buy.

Any gift or incentive program is easy to operate as long as you maintain a checklist or database management program to track revenue acquired from each customer. Keeping your checklist or database program updated monthly lets you know how much merchandise is needed as an incentive.

Motivational Events and Ideas

When thinking about the timing of incentive giving, the first month that may come to mind is December. That's when trinkets of all sizes and styles are distributed. But that's not the sole time of year that items are purchased. I bought my appliance from Sears in May, so it wouldn't have been smart for the salesman to wait for December to send me a thank-you note. You'll find the same to be true in business. There will be reasons to send a client or another person a token of appreciation, such as:

Birthdays. When collecting customer information, ask for the client's birth month. The day is not important because your birthday card, coupon, or small gift is sent at the beginning of the month. It lasts all month long as a reminder of your appreciation. Few companies show gratitude in this manner, so there's room to outshine everyone in your industry.

Referrals. Clients express their loyalty and trust when they recommend your products and services. It's an act worthy of reward. Ask customers how they learn about your company so the correct party benefits from the referrals. Something small, such as a box of truffles or gift card, along with a handwritten note, is appropriate. What you send depends on what you sell.

Contests. Earlier in this chapter you learned about a woman who uses a contest as motivation to open her online newsletter. That's one incentive example. Others include in-shop contests to increase store traffic and inventory turnover and radio partnerships that award prizes to listeners.

Productivity. Incentives encourage everyone who represents your business on a commission basis to sell more within a certain time frame. Additional quantities may be purchased by existing customers, or the reps may elect to find new clients who will benefit from the item or service. In all cases the incentive must match the revenue. No one is eager to receive steak knives if they sell $10,000 in merchandise.

Anniversaries. Your database management software is capable of logging any type of information required, and that includes the month when a client made his first purchase. Sending anniversary gifts is appropriate in this situation, especially for leased items and recurring bills for maintenance and other service.

Good and bad news. Did a client or spouse recently give birth? Did she win an award? Is the client's industry under investigation because of another business? Cards, small gifts by mail when appropriate, and personal phone calls act as incentives. Most companies only make contact when there's something new to sell or when a bill is overdue. Showing support during positive or unfortunate events elevates your relationship to ally rather than being considered as just a salesperson. It's a gesture that goes beyond service.

What's appropriate to spend for incentives and gifts? As a small business owner, naturally you want to keep as much profit as possible, because that's what heightens your success. You can focus on your financial goals and still buy valuable incentives for customers at the same time. For example, if a customer has purchased $100 in merchandise, you may elect to spend between 3 to 7 percent of that total on a gift. That amount might seem small, but there are more than pens and pencils that fit within that price range. When attending trade shows and reviewing advertising magazines, you'll see customized notepads and books, soft carrying cases, desk accessories, edible products, and more. Best of all, each item can be packaged to make a great presentation and appear to be worth a lot more than its cost.

Earlier I mentioned chocolate boxes filled with espresso beans that I gave during the holidays to corporate clients. They not only spent thousands of dollars with me during the year, but some also ordered that same gift for their clients. This shows how your choice of gift sometimes pays for itself, turning an incentive into a profitable investment.

When I began selling products at business and consumer shows, I wanted on-site customers to take something with them as a reminder. That gift was a four-by-six-inch, fifty-page notepad. It stated, "Thanks for your order" at the top and was customized with my business name, address, and telephone number at the bottom (websites and e-mail addresses didn't exist). Extras pads that weren't distributed at shows were sent by mail to customers who ordered a certain amount of products or services that year, along with a personalized pen. I chose not to send an edible product because a usable item would stay in front of each person longer than an open-and-eat gift.

As the years progressed I continued to search for something new and different that was useful in an office or on the road, whatever qualified as clever and beneficial. One product sent to clients was an eyeglass case. It sounds bland, but these cases resemble miniature purses. Colors in swirl, circle, and croco patterns adorned each case, and the soft fabric lining could house a pair of eyeglasses, sunglasses, or any item that fit within the case. Male clients received the same item in gender-pleasing patterns.

Another group received a card initiating them into a membership club where they were allowed to call my office for either a six- or twelve-month time frame to ask questions regarding their businesses. The business-card-size membership card included instructions for use, conditions, expiration date, and value. The last part is very important so that clients understand the cost of service.

Such an incentive is well within your budget. This card was made in the early years of my business using business card stationery sold in office supply stores. Now the card is printed by an online stationery supplier. When clients call for consultation, the questions and answers boost your marketing campaign to sell more services. Restate the problem and solution in whatever format you choose: website FAQs, e-newsletter format, videos, teleseminars, or proprietary information added to print literature available for sale. This proves that your thirty-minute consultation is time well spent, turning the session into another piece of marketing expertise.

SoloMarketingBook.com

Member, Marketing Care Club – 2013

Members receive a complimentary thirty-minute consultation per month with Shirley George Frazier to discuss business problems and solutions.

By e-mail:

mcc@solomarketingbook.com. Subject Line: SBMC 2013.

By telephone:

(555) 555-5555. Mention your club membership.

Thirty minutes per month. Unused minutes cannot be combined or carried over. All questions and answers may be used to create print or audio products. Nontransferable.

Expires 12/31/13. Value $8,000.00.

Where to Find Gifts and Incentives

You may think that the above ideas are the ones to include in your marketing plan, but there are still other incentive items to consider. Thankfully, there is an entire industry dedicated to incentive marketing for you to explore. Since we home-based and solo business owners can't travel around the world in search of the perfect incentive gift, this chapter examines four sources of incentive products, most of which can be accessed from your office chair. One of them will be your choice to create and strengthen client connections.

Magazines

Three trade magazines—*Incentive, Premium Incentive Products (PIP)*, and *Chief Marketer* —highlight incentive trends, surveys, and the latest products that motivate clients to buy and employees to be more productive. Each information magazine is published monthly. The key areas within each publication that help you understand what's available in the incentive market are:

Articles and case studies. Long-format stories explain dilemmas that occur within the business world and how companies find and implement solutions. Many if not all stories focus on large corporations and meeting planner groups layered with management. Still, you will uncover details to transfer into your one-person business.

Columns. Look for sections with quick-to-read ideas that are universal to all businesses. These columns are usually highlighted throughout the magazine with colorful backgrounds that draw attention to the page.

Products. Since these magazines favor incentive items, you'll find photographs of objects throughout each publication, along with contact names and addresses or an insert card to mail for more information. Some favorite incentive items are gift cards, foods and beverages, travel accessories, and electronics. Some items won't fit in your budget; others will seem just right.

Trade magazines aren't available at retail newsstands. However, there are two ways to find these publications:

Visit trade shows that you qualify to attend. *Incentive, Premium Incentive Products,* and *Chief Marketer* are found at incentive-based shows, but they may also be available at your industry's trade shows. Publishers usually promote their magazines at nonindustry shows to help increase readership. Trade shows you visit may display other incentive-based magazines that are not mentioned here.

Subscribe online. Magazine websites, which are discussed next, allow potential subscribers to complete a subscription request form. The form asks if you are the person who makes buying decisions, how much is spent on incentive purchases, the types of incentives purchased, and from whom they're purchased. If you qualify, your subscription will soon arrive by mail.

Incentive **magazine:** www.incentivemag.com
Premium Incentive Products: www.pipmag.com
Chief Marketer: www.chiefmarketer.com

Best of all, these magazines are free of charge to anyone who qualifies for a subscription. That's true for most trade publications. Every trade magazine within the gift industry is complimentary except for *Gifts & Decorative Accessories,* which is the oldest and most respected, giving it the right to charge a price for the thick, monthly publication. If you review a trade magazine and want to subscribe, do your research. Even if you see a subscription charge within its pages, there is a good chance that you can receive the publication gratis. Call the magazine's toll-free number to learn how you can qualify for a complimentary subscription.

Magazine Websites

Each day my postal mailbox overflows with letters, magazines, journals, and advertising specialty products mentioned in this chapter. Companies promote their incentive pens, pads, and calendars by sending samples to home-based and solo businesses. My daily mail can take an hour or more to review.

Perhaps your day follows the same routine, and you don't want another subscription arriving by mail. If that's true, then reviewing a publication's online content is for you. Many articles found in the printed publication are posted on the magazine's website, supplemented by links to product sources and articles from past issues. You can read the information on your computer screen or table or print the articles to read offline.

Having access to materials from back issues is a plus. The publication's website acts as an idea bank, storing relevant articles that you bookmark online rather than pile on your office floor. Here's what else you'll find on the Internet site that's not readily available in the print version:

- Program guides that explain how to create and execute an incentive program for reps, individuals, and corporate clients.
- Links to thousands of suppliers, all grouped by category, selling every imaginable incentive product on the market.
- An editorial calendar listing future topics in case you wish to submit information that promotes your business, or order a print copy that discusses a particular subject in detail.
- Reports outlining why and when to give luxury items, gift cards, certificates, and more.
- Subscription to each publication's online newsletter. Be sure to opt out of any additional e-mail contact that you do not require. If advertisers' e-mails suddenly begin appearing, seemingly as a result of your subscription, visit your account link online to opt out of extraneous subscriptions.
- Links to other free-of-charge magazine websites owned by the publishing group.

Update your monthly tasks to include checking magazine websites once each month to learn new ideas and procedures created by companies that use incentives to boost their revenue.

Trade Shows

Magazines and their websites tell you all about products that promote customer loyalty. Trade shows bring the products up close and personal, letting you see and touch items that exhibitors want you to consider adding to your incentive program. In chapter 8 we looked at these shows from a security angle. But that's not the focus if you're on the buying side of the table. That's the position where you'll find information, fun, and freebies, all waiting for you at shows held throughout the world.

Like trade magazines, trade shows are free of charge. Each show features a keynote speaker who shares his message before the show begins. When the presentation ends, the show doors open, and throngs of eager buyers squeeze through a space controlled by security officials who ensure that you are wearing a badge that admits you into the show. Anyone who's attended in the past knows that the earlier you arrive, the more freebies you collect. Exhibitors tend to run out of samples when buyers spot a giveaway frenzy. The samples are items personalized with the exhibitors' name and logo. A sample is something to take away from the booth after speaking with a representative—although you'll watch some buyers grab and run as if they fear the exhibitors.

Incentive product trade shows sound as though the focus is on getting free samples. That's the activity for a small percentage of attendees. For you, the event will provide a meaningful look at ways in which to reward clients for their loyalty, to thank referrals for new customer recommendations, and to convince prospects to start a new relationship with your business.

The Motivation Show: www.motivationshow.com
Rewards & Recognition Expo: www.nyirr.com

Frame a plan of action before attending a show. Walking in with no plan or budget won't gain you anything except wasted time from the office. Here's what to consider:

1. What do you hope to achieve? Set clear goals, such as finding products within one or several price ranges, learning about product customization options, and speaking with representatives who will guide you through the entire incentive ordering process.

2. What is the average merchandise price you're willing to pay per client? This is determined by calculating how much the average client spends on your products and services. As mentioned earlier, most companies stay within a 3 to 7 percent range of that average. If clients spend approximately $200 per sale, then a reward priced from $6 to $14 is acceptable. Also consider any norms within your industry that adjust this percentage higher or lower.

3. Which companies listed in the preshow directory will you visit? Scan the online or printed list of exhibitors. You will see brand names known worldwide and smaller firms that are unfamiliar. Companies that are unknown but that have names that sound intriguing are likely to have websites for further review. Examine the preshow list carefully and decide which booths to visit. The show operates for at least three days, but in this planning stage, your mission is to make sure you visit specific exhibitors with products that match your needs. Companies not on your list often exhibit merchandise you had not considered. Those booths are bonuses when you're searching for something special.

4. What seminars will you attend? All seminars are generally free, as is the keynote presentation. Review the seminar topics and times. Add to your calendar any lectures that promise to share valuable information. Seminars offer a chance to meet other seminar attendees if you practice your networking skills (see chapter 2).

5. Where else can you visit, related to business or fun, while in town? Whether the trade show is located in your town or in another state or country, you want to make the most of your time out of the office. Websites, preshow planners, and hotel concierges help you find other places to visit for business or fun. Museums, bookstores, and outdoor events are instrumental to refresh your mind and provide new perspective on problems and solutions, so look for these facilities while away.

Be aware of how much material you carry at the show. You will receive a show bag to fill with literature, and exhibitors will also offer bags, but all that paper and giveaway merchandise will become heavy. If you're thinking of bringing a wheeled cart with you, think again. Many shows prohibit these carts on the show floor because they can be tripping hazards. Check the preshow directory to see if wheeled carts are allowed. Better yet, opt to carry only what you want to review when returning to the office, and give your business card to exhibitors to send by mail those materials that you don't need to examine immediately.

Trade Show Directories

Every trade and consumer show publishes a buyers' directory, available free of charge to all attendees. It lists all exhibitors, names the show management staff, describes other shows produced by the group, and displays advertisements purchased by exhibitors who believe that the extra promotion will increase sales. What's most relevant is the information provided about each exhibitor, including:

- Address
- Toll-free number
- Website and e-mail addresses
- Booth location (important when searching for an exhibitor whose booth number changed from what's shown in the preshow directory)
- Exhibit booth representatives' names
- Description of products and services

This information can be vital when searching for names and merchandise not found in trade show magazines. Some companies focus their marketing dollars on trade show booths rather than buy ad space in publications, so there can be differences in each type of literature.

Directories give you a complete look at the conference. Ordering the directory provides a guided tour of the event when you're unable to attend. In most cases directory copies are available when the show ends. Management offices are happy to send you one for a fee. One popular gourmet food trade show prices its directory at $30.

Before ordering a directory, ask colleagues if they plan to attend a show or if they are physically located near the show. One of them may pick up an extra copy while there and mail it to you soon after. I do this for industry friends on the West Coast who cannot attend East Coast shows. We help each other in many ways, so we don't charge each other for postage. This gratis arrangement keeps all of us armed with information needed to stay up to date within our industry.

I also offer this directory-sharing option to clients in certain industries who, for whatever reason, cannot travel to a show. When cosmetic, fashion, accessories, and furniture conferences that I attend are held in the New York City area, I call clients in those industries to find out if they wish to receive a directory. That's part of the customer service I provide to keep our relationship strong, and it's another reason why they won't migrate to a competitor. It's a point to keep in mind when you visit shows or if shows that affect your clients' longevity arrive in your area. What competing firm in your industry provides this type of service to their clients?

Show directories are catalogued in my office library. As the shelf fills, I take one last look at older directories to make sure I've removed any information that must be kept. Then I throw away old editions to make space for the new. Be sure to review your directories in the same manner, compiling information from them to create specialty directories discussed in chapter 6.

Incentive Products That Increase Loyalty

Companies exhibiting at trade shows display a wide assortment of products. One side of the show features smaller companies launching incentive merchandise for the first time. On the other side are well-known firms selling items in higher-priced categories. Both groups of gift ideas are important, as all buyers need to make wise choices when rewarding clients. Here are some examples taken directly from the shows that I've attended to give you an idea of what's available and how to evaluate what to buy.

Miniature Foldout Maps

This item is attractive and handy for companies that allow clients to visit their location, and it provides much more than just directions. The map folds small enough to put into a pocket or wallet. When opened, one side contains an actual map of the business's location, guiding the client or visitor to a physical address. On the other side, each folded section contains any type of information you can imagine. Tips are printed in one square, a coupon is in another, and a list of important industry dates occupies two squares. Each area is filled according to the business's requirements. Map manufacturers create this item to your specifications. You then distribute the product, which acts as a customized service to complement your marketing plan.

Home-based and solo business owners' offices aren't always accessible to clients. What if you want a foldout map but have no use for the map portion? You might replace the map with industry facts and figures or important industry locations. The product was designed to be a map, but suppliers are happy to work with you to create your perfect incentive item.

Tickets to DINE-IN Theaters

Your customers are tireless workers. They rarely make time for themselves. Casual conversations reveal their appreciation for fiction books, adventure, and getting away from the office. Sending them tickets for a night at the movies, refreshments included, will keep your business on their minds and in turn they refer lots of new business to you.

Every theater chain offers an incentive program to distribute movie and refreshment tickets. The cost of movies today makes this item a thrill for people who enjoy the big-screen environment but not the expense. This incentive package costs less than retail, but to your clients, it will seem as though you've spent a million dollars.

Buying movie tickets has its downside. Not every client will have a particular theater chain in their area, especially if she lives in a rural setting versus a metropolis. If you purchase tickets for one chain, and the closest one is fifty miles away, that may impose a hardship on clients who will either not use the tickets or give them to someone else. Your incentive loses its luster, and so does the possibility of added income or referral business.

If tickets are the right option, this gift of rest, relaxation, fun, and laughter will make clients very happy to call you a business ally and friend.

Bottled Water with Custom Labels

The occasional backlash against buying bottled water may make you hesitate to consider this idea, but your bottles are likely to be handed directly to clients or distributed free of charge at a worthy event. Additionally, consider pairing your business name with an eco-friendly campaign. Donate a portion of any proceeds you receive through on-site and future sales to a charity that's linked with the earth's preservation.

Be sure to display a sign about the charitable partnership next to your bottled water, and promote sponsorships on event banners. This kind of signage is not typically used by large corporations simply because they are not required to display it. As a solo marketer, posting such signs reaffirms your commitment to the community and the environment, two important considerations in your long-term success.

Edibles

Chocolate, cookie, pizza, popcorn, steak, and seafood manufacturers and distributors create tasty assortments packaged to perfection. Small boxes containing two truffles show appreciation on a small scale when there's no need for a twenty-piece box. Popcorn is delivered in microwavable bags customized with your name and logo or in large pails of ready-to-eat flavors with your company's name displayed on the lid. Firms specializing in combining fruits and foods into gift baskets and boxes are located worldwide. Also consider restaurant certificates for a night of steak and seafood, courtesy of your firm.

Everyone must eat, so if an edible product is selected as an incentive, you'll find a wealth of food products to choose from at trade shows, in magazines, and on websites. Most companies offer programs that send gifts directly to your clients or to you for distribution. Before deciding on what to order, you must know clients' preferences—and even their food allergies, dietary restrictions, and flavor distinctions. Which clients eat nuts, and which do not? Is a customer who will receive chocolates maintaining a strict reducing plan? These are some of the questions to answer before sending edible incentives.

The popularity of food gifts keeps this incentive within the top-ten choices worldwide. Select the right gift so you are seen in your clients' eyes as a top-ten business provider. As with the movie tickets, try not to present the client with an edible that he will turn around and redistribute due to dietary restrictions. Make sure your choice will be enjoyed and remembered long after it's consumed.

Electronics

This category is led by Apple-manufactured products, cameras, and televisions. However, there's more to the electronics group: Desk and alarm clocks, DVD players, and spy technology are part of the category. All are affordable incentives if purchased as part of the 3 to 7 percent sales budget. Digital cameras make a wonderful gift, and many suppliers allow you to customize the packaging. Some watches also fit this category, although watches may be considered too personal an item for clients.

If electronics fit into your incentive planning, it's best to stick with general-use products for the office or travel. Many exhibitors display electronics at trade shows. Most products are in a glass cabinet for inspection, and you'll need a representative's help for a closer look.

Although the electronics mentioned here are considered affordable for the one-person office's budget, it is the large corporate clients that these manufacturers court at trade shows. DVD players, flat panel televisions, and iPads are coveted gifts added to prize packages for "the most productive employee," "the salesman with earnings of one million dollars in a quarter," and other outstanding achievements. The incentive product must match the results. This is the same for your clients. The higher the sales investment, the more expensive the incentive gift, within reason.

Internal Revenue Service (IRS) rules for US-based businesses state that "you can deduct no more than $25 for business gifts you give directly or indirectly to any one person during your tax year." So while it is acceptable to buy an incentive that is worth more than $25, this amount is the limit you can deduct for tax purposes. The word "acceptable" brings many questions to mind. Is it acceptable to give a client an expensive watch or a camera? Is it appropriate to bestow luxury items? Home-based businesses tend to shy away from such incentives. Clients may perceive the gift as not only expensive but also as an item that, if not purchased, would have reduced their invoice. It's good to know that there are plenty of incentive products that stay within the IRS rules and your own budget.

There's nothing stopping you from buying pens, pencils, letter openers, and other well-known, low-cost specialty products. These items succeed in situations where you need to give away a specialty item but want it to cost as little as possible while the value is considered as high.

Men-specific incentives include tools, outdoor accessories, and sports memorabilia in product or gift card form. Office supply stores and electronics retailers offer gift cards in various price categories. Three categories to choose very selectively are personal care accessories, smoking products, and barware. Such items might not be appropriate for your incentives list unless you know, beyond a shadow of a doubt, that these are the clients' gift of choice.

Incentive Marketing Ideas

There are times when it's appropriate to tell clients about buying incentives. In other cases no notification is needed, such as end-of-year giving or other times within the year when incentive gifts are dispersed. The Center for Concept Development, Ltd. documented the top methods for alerting customers about gift and incentive programs as:

1. Advertising (print or electronic)
2. E-mail/direct mail letter (tie)
3. Word of mouth
4. Internet/social media

5. Store displays/signs
6. Newsletter

Businesses that sell in any environment are able to promote effectively using one or more of these categories. For example, a retail store owner uses signs posted on windows and throughout the shop to notify customers about free tote bags filled with merchandise given as an incentive when buying from the store. This owner also mails postcards to clients on his mailing list, and if he has a website, the incentive offer is posted there as well.

A home-based retailer with no walk-in store uses some of the same marketing techniques, but she can incorporate other ideas. Her gift-with-a-purchase incentive is posted front and center on her website and social media pages, and a reminder is added on the secure shopping cart's main page. The signature line in her e-mails announces the event, and postcards are mailed to current and past clients. Bagged merchandise accompanies this retailer to a consumer trade show where on-site buyers receive the incentive with purchase. This giveaway creates lots of traffic around her booth and encourages more sales. Her online newsletter also mentions the event, and statistics show higher traffic on her website and more sales for the month than the same month last year when no incentive was available.

Service-based business owners benefit from similar techniques depending on the industry, collaborations, and ideas gained through networking. An interior designer's incentive offered with the purchase of home window treatments is featured on a postcard or flyer that accompanies services mailed to prospects by a successful real estate agent. Accountants generally don't need to offer incentives, but those who are just starting or relaunching their businesses might offer a free evaluation. That's what CPA Janet Ross (chapter 1) is considering as she expands. She plans to mention this free evaluation when speaking at luncheon events and networking with potential clients at breakfast and dinner meetings.

Certain industries offer no incentives. Plumbers, pest control, mechanics, electricians, doctors, and dentists are service providers who rarely need to distribute gifts of any type to gain your patronage. But these professionals must include basic marketing in their overall business plan to increase their client list and generate additional revenue.

Incentives bring attention to companies looking for a promotional boost, but offering incentives on too regular a basis may impede your growth. Buyers are notorious for becoming conditioned to waiting for an incentive offer. All of a sudden, gifts that were once popular are no longer special. This is why smart solo business owners offer incentives as part of their yearly promotional plan, not part of everyday business.

Rewarding customers who deliver a generous portion of business and referral clients produces a steady stream of revenue all year long. Choose incentives that match your clients' preferences. Then add their words of gratitude to your print literature, website, and social media pages (with permission) to continue the marketing cycle.

10 Seven Marketing Methods for Savvy Soloists

This book has introduced numerous business promotion ideas, and each is achievable by you, the solo business owner. You've reviewed marketing plans (chapter 1), uncovered Internet resources (chapter 7), learned how to market by mail (chapter 3), and read about people who took a wrong turn during the marketing process (chapter 2). Thankfully, there are many entrepreneurs who stay on course. This section unveils six affordable marketing ideas that you may not have considered but, as each story explains, may become part of your personal marketing arsenal.

Idea No. 1—Using Accessories to Break the Ice

Wholesalers frequently ask me for advice on new ways to market their products. The industries they serve change often due to consolidations, industry turnovers, and economic conditions. That's true for all industries. If you can depend on one thing, it's change and the constant need to stay updated to serve new and current clients.

One of my wholesale clients supplies her customers with beautiful baskets. Each one is crafted masterfully, similar to works of art. No two baskets include the same handle or weaving technique. Her warehouse is filled from top to bottom with multicolor baskets in all shapes and sizes, organized on tall steel shelves to easily select and ship baskets when customers order.

I called the wholesaler to discuss business ideas, and before we concluded she told me about her plans to visit a grocery store to buy a few items before ending her day. I thought about my supermarket visits and how I bring bags with me for a five-cent credit per bag on each order. Then I asked myself why this wholesaler concerns herself with recycling bags when one of her baskets would not only carry several lightweight items but also serve to market her business?

She quickly realized my idea's merit and choose a basket from her inventory to accompany her on the trip. Although this wholesaler was not a regular seller of single baskets, she knew that her community included people who purchase multiple baskets for hobby or business purposes. The basket would surely generate questions from curious shoppers. Cosmetics consultants, scrapbookers, meeting planners, and others in business for themselves or working for large companies were potential buyers, and they could promote the product through word-of-mouth conversations after seeing the basket on her arm.

Both of us believed that this type of promotion within the store would not be prohibited, because:

1. The basket is in use to hold multiple products, serving the same purpose as the store's carryall.
2. The unlidded basket poses no threat to store security. At checkout, it's wise to turn the basket upside down after the contents are removed to prove that the vessel is empty.
3. The wholesaler is being approached by shoppers; she's not soliciting customers on the store's premises. Store management wants happy buyers and doesn't mind customers gathering for short discussions about an accessory that won't compete with their inventory.

As we talked, I suggested to the basket wholesaler that she take lots of business cards for distribution when shoppers approach her. Creating a second business card, discussed in chapter 2, might prove beneficial to target this alternative market. We both agreed that standing on the checkout line would encourage more interest from other shoppers and the register attendant, as long as she chose a line with a female cashier.

You don't have to sell physical products to use the accessory approach. Lynn Colwell, a life and personal coach and owner of Bloom 'n Grow Coaching for Life based in Washington state, discovered that using accessories to break the ice worked better for her than approaching prospective customers with the uninspiring phrase, "I'm a life coach." Lynn acts as an ancillary partner to her clients, providing them with encouragement and action-oriented instruction to keep their goals on track as they pursue their life's work. Here's how Lynn turned a personal accessory into a business generator.

"I don't usually pursue clients through local networking or marketing because I coach by phone and my clients are located throughout the United States," Lynn explains. "One day I decided to attend a full-day program for women entrepreneurs, many of whom I thought would be interested in my services. The vast majority of women attending this program are in the twenties to early thirties age range. I'm sixty, and because of this I sometimes go unnoticed in a crowd of younger women. I wanted to create a way for these women to approach me rather than my joining conversations in which I might not be welcome.

"I had what turned out to be a brilliant idea. I have several Mary Frances purses. She makes handbags that are true works of art. One cannot ignore a Mary Frances bag. Not only are they breathtaking, they are also conversation starters. I chose a beautiful red purse that guarantees lots of attention and headed off for the day. I carried the bag as conspicuously as I could. One by one, women approached me. I stopped counting after ten of them complimented my bag. This gave me the in I needed to ask about their profession. They, in turn, asked me. From there, I gained their permission to contact them about my complimentary coaching call. Those calls resulted in signing two new clients."

Stress Benefits, Not Titles

Many solo business owners find that describing their profession in terms of what they accomplish for clients, rather than stating their exact job title, encourages interest and more options to gain business. I've worked with clients who announce themselves as "gift retailers" at business functions. That designation tells listeners nothing about the benefit to their personal or professional lives. Gift retailers do more than sell gifts. Their products establish relationships between multimillion-dollar companies or firms that desire to reach that sales level. It's that type of benefit that people attending business functions need to hear when you're asked, "What do you do?" Creating a sentence that tells the benefit of your product or service provides a boost to your marketing strategy.

Idea No. 2—Suitcase Marketing

When traveling by air to conduct seminars, I maximize my time by checking area adult schools to see if there's time to present additional seminars while in town. The seminar will focus on business marketing or gift basket making, two of my specialties. If speaking about gifts, I bring items in my luggage to show attendees how to bundle gifts using cellophane.

Fitting crackers, cheese, cookies, and other goodies in my luggage is time consuming. Each item is packaged separately to minimize damage. This leaves little room for clothing, but I manage to pack everything in one bag. After the seminar I give away all of the goodies to students.

Carrying food items in my luggage makes it an automatic candidate for inspection by the Federal Aviation Administration (FAA). This is where my marketing skills reach a new level. I add two things in my suitcase atop the contents: a handwritten note posted on legal paper, and business cards. The white paper lies flat on top of the luggage contents. One message states:

> *If looking in luggage is not the profession for you, perhaps a career in gift basket design will be more rewarding.*
>
> *GiftBasketBusiness.com holds all the answers to start a successful and profitable business. You have my permission to take a business card posted at the bottom for yourself, a friend, or family member.*
>
> *Wishing you the best that life offers,*
> *Shirley George Frazier*

My message is not written to encourage airline workers to quit their jobs, but it does offer people an option if they are not living up to their potential. Perhaps a relative or friend has expressed a desire to start a business, and gift basket design happens to be a viable option. The answer is in my luggage, and I'm taking the opportunity to market in a nonthreatening manner. Why not use available space to promote another profession's benefits along with offering a business card, postcard, or flyer?

I'm pleased to say that many business cards have been removed, while everything else in the suitcase arrived at its destination with no problem. There's no way to know how many sales I've gained through this type of marketing, as many orders arrive in my online cart without knowledge of how the client found my site. However, as long as I'm able to promote in this manner, I will continue doing so.

Suitcase marketing works whether you're a frequent or sporadic traveler. Your luggage may not always be inspected, but if you must store items during a trip, this option may bring you business as you travel. Here are some tips to make suitcase marketing easy and effective:

- Make sure your message includes an immediate solution that benefits the reader, whether or not the reader is searching for a solution.
- Write your message on legal-size white paper, or letter size if legal paper isn't available or appropriate. Legal paper provides more room for your message.
- Use a black, felt-tip pen. If your handwriting isn't legible, select a large, bold Arial or Times Roman font, as some readers may not be able to read italics and other script fonts.
- Clip business cards or another promotional item to the message. Sticky yellow notes that include your business name, website address, telephone number, and social media address are another option.
- Place the marketing message atop your luggage contents, available for review immediately when opened.

New clients are found in the most restrictive places. If you travel, your luggage has the potential to bring you a customer base that's ready and willing to buy. There's nothing on the FAA list of unacceptable stowed luggage items that prohibits this type of marketing.

Idea No. 3—15 Minutes of Fame through Twitter

If you read stories on the web about how people make life-changing connections on Twitter and say to yourself, "That can't be true," I may have agreed with you if such a connection hadn't happened to me in August 2012. That's the month I began searching for and following television and cable show hosts and similar people with potential to invite me on air.

After brainstorming a list of personal names and show titles that had the highest potential of interest in my expertise, I entered those names into Twitter's search engine, found these notable people, and began following them on my Twitter stream organized through Hootsuite, a free online program that makes it easy to read who's saying what at any given time.

As I read these new tweets, I responded with genuine comments to what each person said. Some of my list tweeted messages that were self-serving ("I'm great; I'm beautiful," etc.), so I stopped following them. Others shared highlights about their upcoming shows, and that's where I concentrated my efforts.

One of my responses to a show tweet made a connection with a host/producer who leads a popular show on an ABC affiliate station. Here's an excerpt from our Twitter conversation through its private message tool (starting with my tweet):

"Glad the show is about shopping deals. Can't wait to watch."

"Wonderful! Where are you located?"

"I'm in the New York City area. Can I assist you in finding something?"

"Do you ever visit Dallas?"

"I have travelled there and expect to return very soon."

"We'll soon tape a segment on holiday gift baskets and would like to include you. Can you come to Dallas?"

"Sounds great. I'm sure I can join you. What's your taping schedule?"

Our discussion continued by e-mail, as we needed more than Twitter's 140-character limit to finalize the arrangements for the segment. About one month later, I boarded an airplane to Dallas, Texas, and met the producer the next day at a retail store decorated with festive merchandise and accessories, a perfect backdrop for the holiday broadcast.

The taping was complete in three hours, and before returning home by plane the next day, I celebrated by enjoying a great meal and writing down preliminary plans to market the segment before, during, and after the airing.

Before agreeing to this or any opportunity, you must calculate the cost and determine if, in the long run, such marketing is worth the investment. The total cost for all expenses was $502. That's lower than most online and print marketing when compared to the results this segment will deliver as it's seen worldwide during the initial airing and shown in perpetuity on my own site and blog, social media, YouTube, and the broadcaster's and its affiliates' stations and websites.

My advice is for you to make Twitter your connection to people who will provide you with local, regional, and international exposure. To date, it's the only social media program where users read what you share, and in doing so, learn more about you and hopefully invite you to join them in whatever manner spreads your valuable message.

Brainstorm a list of people in your industry, in broadcasting, and on satellite radio who have the capability of delivering your message to a wide audience. Follow their tweets, respond when appropriate, and remember to deliver great messages of your own to encourage your newfound alliances to follow you back. When other people learn that you made your broadcast connection through Twitter, they'll also think, "That can't be true," while you'll know that this and much more in the marketing world is possible.

Idea No. 4—Using Gifts to Produce Results

Remember the story about the teacup and saucer in chapter 5? Creating that gift was the first time I presented such an item to another person to market my business. Thankfully, the technique worked, but it doesn't always succeed. I've sent door-opening gifts to Realtors in an attempt to collaborate on thank-you gifts for their clients, to NBC's *The Today Show* to turn my expertise into an on-air appearance, and to a radio executive to try and extend our relationship. All of that failed. Nonetheless, include gift giving as part of your marketing plan whenever possible—and appropriate.

There are times when gifts are appropriate and other times when they are prohibited. Pursuing a prospect who works in the private sector (his or her own business, for example) is suitable, but sending a gift to thank a person in any type of media (television, radio, newspapers, etc.) or law enforcement profession is improper, as it is viewed as a bribe or favoritism. One impression you never want to leave is one of embarrassment. Let conversations with colleagues, information in books and blogs, and the Internet resources keep you updated on gift giving dos and don'ts before deciding how to dazzle the prospect.

Although members of the media usually don't accept gifts, there are exceptions. You must be an industry participant to know and play by the rules. Roz Miller Choice worked as a freelance broadcaster for eighteen years. Like many solo business owners, she succeeded in a number of industries before finding her life's work in New Jersey as a real estate investor. Her story takes marketing to new levels. I'll let her explain.

"Theater was my major in college, but I soon changed my professional outlook when I realized that an acting career might be spotty. So I decided to go into a profession (broadcasting) that I hoped would provide more consistency.

"I grew up in Brooklyn. Surprisingly and thankfully, my broadcasting career began in New York City. This job was with WNYC-TV, a public television station. My job was covering Ed Koch, then mayor of New York, in early 1984. It was a volunteer job, and I was a writer working for no salary.

"After that position I went on to join other New York market TV stations. In the beginning I was a general assignment reporter covering crime, politics, and human interest. I enjoyed the variety. No two days were the same. One day I'd interview Nelson Mandela or the president of another country. The next day I'd report a water main break while standing in three feet of water.

"The broadcasting industry is a hidden job market. You cannot buy the *New York Times* to find an ad for a reporter's job. This industry is all about networking. You have to talk with other reporters to find work. You also hear about jobs from engineers, cameramen, and others in the business. The news director often makes the decision as to who will conduct on-air reporting, and the only way on-camera talent is contracted is through sending a videotape or DVD. Résumés are tossed if not accompanied by a demo.

"I was not contracted to one particular station. As a solo freelancer, it's your job to find your work, so you can be working for three or four stations simultaneously. I wrote news for WNBC Channel 4 in New York while I provided the New York Fox Station with on-air reporting. I cohosted a travel show on New Jersey Network and worked for stations that aired throughout the world, including an assignment as a New York correspondent for CNN. Many reporters hire agents who do the marketing to find them jobs. In my eighteen years as a freelance reporter, I found much more work than an agent could find for me.

"After spending years as a reporter, I decided it was time to produce special shows. To convince television stations and show sponsors to partner with me on a segment about breast cancer, I had to do something outstanding to get their attention. Breast cancer's symbol is a pink ribbon, but instead of ribbons I ordered dozens of pink flowers for delivery to television stations and proposed sponsors. This marketing plan generated many responses, including a meeting with the Susan G. Komen organization to talk about the potential show. My plan faded, but for good reason—a production company and I teamed up to work on a show for the themed restaurant Planet Hollywood.

"My most costly marketing project is one that led me to my current profession. My plan was to produce home improvement shows, and to prove my passion for this project, I bought a three-family house through a government auction. The house was in major disrepair. A production company worked with me to videotape the renovation project as it moved through the before, during, and after stages. Program directors received the video, which I wrapped in a brown leather-and-suede tool belt containing screwdrivers, electrical tape, a 5-in-1 tool, and other products. This garnered responses from every target. One California television producer was very interested and we discussed creating a show for me. Oddly, instead of the project leading me to home improvement shows, it exposed my talent as a real estate investor."

Roz skillfully employed marketing tactics to attract attention throughout her journey from reporting to real estate. As a freelancer she understood what was necessary to get the desired results. Roz shares one final story about a marketing strategy that I helped her fulfill in the mid-1990s and that continues to pay off today.

"I'm big on saying thank you. A colleague did something very special for me, and I wanted to show my appreciation. I called Shirley. She created a gift basket using a top hat and sent it to him. He received it and was overwhelmed with joy.

"This colleague started a television production company in Manhattan, and it's been successful for more than ten years. He continues to call me to do television production work for him, all because of that gift sent so many years ago. I continue to get business from him because he connects me with that good feeling he experienced opening his gift basket."

Idea No. 5—Specialty Regional Websites and Publications

Occasional trips to meetings or for research in or outside of your state or country allow you to form fresh perspectives about business as you are stimulated by the new environment. The time away can be used in another productive form, as illustrated by this habit I developed when traveling.

First, I search online for websites with information on business and casual events. This is a must when going to a conference where you will be out of town for several days. Your main focus is getting the most from the conference, but any downtime can be converted into an opportunity to mingle with people or visit places that aren't readily available at home.

Online newspapers and magazines and specialty websites list events at museums, bookstores, and other public facilities. You will also find business gatherings where visitors are welcomed, such as chamber of commerce events, dinner meetings, and evening mixers.

Finding these websites takes little time as long as you use proper search engine keywords. I search for newspapers by typing "(state name) newspapers" in quotes in any search engine. A list of major publications will appear, as well as weeklies, some of which provide more information on local events than well-known newspapers. This type of search proves extremely helpful in areas outside of metropolitan towns such as New York City, Chicago, Atlanta, Dallas, and Los Angeles.

Specialty magazines also make navigation easy when visiting small and large towns. They are often free of charge, referred to as "throwaways," and can be found in town supermarkets, street corner newspaper-dispensing machines, restaurants, conference centers, and airports. When I visit Chicago I'll consult the *Today's Chicago Woman* website, and if there's time, I'll also look for the magazine's hard copy in a dispensing machine on South Michigan Avenue.

Once you review many of these "throwaways," you'll wonder, as I do, why they carry this designation. Some do not provide information that matches your interests, but others supply a wealth of insightful articles, advice, and case studies not found in your home publications. You'll also find a roster of events happening the same time you're in town. Thanks to a regional publication, a profitable business idea might be waiting for you at a local breakfast meeting in a city you're visiting that day.

Consulting these event sources online is part of my out-of-office preparation. However, if I know I'll return to the same area within a year, these publications work to provide ideas for revenue. For example, papers in dispensing machines inform me about community colleges and area learning centers with programs that allow experts to educate the general public about a certain topic. Months before returning to Las Vegas, for example, I scheduled a seminar through a community college and generated $2,000 in speaking fees and sales within two hours. Similar results occurred during trips to Denver and to Portland, Maine. In-class marketing of my reports, CDs, website, and membership club encourages more sales in the future. This additional revenue occurs because I planned to be in town for one event and decided to reap rewards from another opportunity. If you have a topic that's presentable in a class format, whether to consumers or business owners, the same approach is open to you if you make research and planning part of your trip preparation.

Third, I visit state chamber of commerce and travel and tourism department websites. Chambers usually charge a fee for nonmembers, but if the subject allows for better marketing opportunities, the investment is worth the cost. Each website lists events in different formats, but most display an overview of conventions and other gatherings throughout each US state. You may not qualify to attend all these gatherings, but if you can get to an event's facility, specialty publications may be available in the lobby with news and other insights about the industry.

Do you still wonder how searching through specialty publications and websites strengthens your marketing plan? Here are six benefits:

1. Networking with people outside of your regular circles opens you to ideas previously not considered.
2. Reading where business owners conduct events and seminars provides a new perspective on how to gather prospects and clients to hear your message.
3. Reviewing solutions to business problems uncovers answers to your own dilemmas and those experienced by clients.
4. Finding new publications lets you share the discovery with associates and clients. This a) makes them search their memory for similar publications to reciprocate ideas, and b) secures your relationship as a business ally, putting you atop their list of people to contact first when a business opportunity arises.
5. Uncovering competitive companies' websites, mentioned in these publications, helps you keep a watchful eye on their businesses.
6. Analyzing potential clients through insightful articles gives you an advantage when approaching them to offer your services.

Regional websites and publications aid your business growth, or they work to keep your options strong within a tight niche. Not all locations will have a comprehensive regional site, but each area will have a newspaper with business and/or casual offerings that often lead you to additional listings.

Idea No. 6—Preparing for Your Close-up

Time magazine publishes a special year-end issue of best photos. In 2011, photographs memorializing the tenth anniversary of 9/11, Japan's devastating tsunami and earthquake, flowers on Elizabeth Taylor's Hollywood Walk of Fame star, and unrests in Libya and Yemen topped their list. These pictures remind you of events that are easily forgotten as months pass unless you, your business, or family members share a direct connection.

Photo galleries are not exclusive to *Time*. Home-based business owners can create their own best photos galleries to post on websites, on blogs, and in marketing materials. Have a camera on hand each time products or services are delivered, seminars and speeches are conducted, interns are trained, sponsorships are awarded, and donations are fulfilled. When you capture these memories photographically as part of marketing, you can show prospects and clients how your business impacts others personally and professionally. Digital photos are your first choice, but disposable cameras need not be overlooked if a digital camera isn't available.

Flora Morris Brown, PhD, knows all about capturing memorable pictures to boost her business. She teaches critical thinking at Fullerton College in California and promotes self-book publishing on her website ColorYourLifePublished.com. Flora's teaching roots began on the junior high school level. That passion for education led her to open a Los Angeles–based reading and math tutoring program. As she created the program from scratch, Flora knew that it would take a healthy dose of marketing to get the attention her program deserved. Here's how she put her plan in focus.

"I started thinking about a tutoring program when I was a junior high school reading teacher," Flora recounts. "The students needed a concentrated reading program, and I was frustrated that the system didn't create something intensive enough for them. I didn't want to run an entire school, but the children needed extra help, so I decided to focus on a private reading and math program.

"The plan began to develop when I resigned from the junior high school system and returned to the University of Southern California." When Flora completed her PhD, she launched the school inside a private preschool that her youngest child attended. Then she moved the part-time program to a church with an educational center.

"The program was so popular that I decided to run it full-time from my home's two-car garage, which was completely remodeled into a space with a classroom, small reception area, and lavatory. It housed a receptionist, teachers, and the students.

In time the garage became too cramped. I could not schedule testing for incoming students because testing was being performed in the same space where students were being tutored. A bigger building was needed to accommodate everyone, so I purchased a commercial building in Los Angeles, just fourteen blocks from my home. I thought to myself, 'I have to get more serious to promote a larger program.'

"My marketing campaign started with trifold brochures I made and distributed to the parents at my child's preschool. I advertised in a throwaway paper called Southwest Wave. It contained local news, a food section with great recipes, and a church section. The price for a three-line ad was cheap, and it connected me with lots of paying parents. I also succeeded at having my program included on university referral lists. Universities often have these lists for parents looking for tutoring services.

"I met a photographer through a friend. He was a photojournalist, a person who snapped pictures of news as it happened. He encouraged me to write press releases, which became part of my marketing.

"I watched and read the news, looking for dignitaries who would be in town. When I saw something of interest, I called the photographer and asked him to meet me at the event so I could have my photograph taken with the famous person. The photojournalist taught me how to pose and how to help him get good pictures. I had to be assertive when going after my photos. Crowds form around these dignitaries, but I know I must get my picture. Thank goodness this opportunity occurred before today's security concerns. I was able to approach the person and shake his or her hand. Then I'd ask, 'Is it okay if I take a picture with you?' They always approved.

"The photographer and I worked as a team. I would shake the person's hand and tell them where to look. I made sure we were both face forward so it looked like the person was shaking my hand legitimately. The photographer developed eight-by-ten-inch black-and-white photos. I wrote the photo caption, which read similar to 'Dr. Flora Brown, director of the Morris-Brown Reading Academy, greets (person's name) at (location).' Then I hand delivered the picture to the Southwest Wave. Some of the dignitaries who appeared in the newspaper posing with me were the Rev. Jesse Jackson, former Los Angeles mayor Tom Bradley, and California congresswoman Diane Watson."

This local marketing also netted Flora an article in the *Los Angeles Times* and a live segment on a news broadcast. She encourages anyone who wants to pursue this type of photo promotion to work with a professional photographer. "Celebrities move fast through a crowd, so you will only have a few seconds and just one chance to get a great still photo. If you work with an amateur, you may not get the shot you want in a timely manner."

Idea No. 7—Vehicle Marketing

Many home-based business owners, including me, use their personal vehicles as rolling billboards. It's a popular method to market while on the road. Anything from a business name to website address is fair game to advertise, depending on the information targeted for marketing and the space required for the message. It's an idea that large corporations and radio stations take one step further by enveloping buses and vans in one gigantic ad. Even the vehicles' windows are coated on the outside, but riders see no trace of it on the inside. One-person businesses, for the most part, haven't elected to spray coat their vehicles in this manner, but there are numerous options for effective marketing while we travel.

I owned a minivan when I began my business. It ensured plenty of room for my gifts as I traveled to corporate presentations and trade shows. My first vehicle sign was made by an office supply company selling its products by catalog. The sign was magnetic (similar to what plumbers, electricians, and real estate agents still use today), placed on the driver's door just below the window. Its white background allowed the black lettering of my company's name, slogan, and telephone number to stand out.

Before buying the sign, I consulted with an attorney to determine if this type of advertisement put my company in jeopardy if an accident occurred. He assured me that any lawsuits would be of a personal nature, not business, because the vehicle did not carry commercial license plates. This is a question to ask your attorney if you choose to place a sign on your vehicle; your region may have different laws and statutes.

I remember feeling self-conscious the first time the sign appeared on the van. People stared at me while waiting at a red light. After a few weeks, telephone calls arrived asking about my products. Some callers said they saw the information on my car sign, so it was working as a promotional tool. More calls and sales resulted in additional income. Years passed, and the van decided to cease operation. Another car took its place, and I needed a new sign.

A visitor on a small business Internet message board mentioned a plastic sign he used on his car. It clung to the inside back windshield, allowing anyone in back of or passing the car to see his message. This seemed to be a sturdy, more weatherproof product than a magnetic sign. I searched the web and found a supplier of clear, plastic advertising signs, also known as decals, that adhere easily to a vehicle's clean windshield. The sign's background color was clear, but the customized phrase was written in black and outlined in white. I purchased two decals in the late 1990s for under $40. The decals grip sturdily and won't move as long as the entire plastic is pressed onto the window. The product is strong enough to withstand rough handling and is as light as a feather when held in your hand.

I've placed one sign inside my car, where it stays in place unless I move it. The other sign is reserved for use in rental cars. It folds easily, and I place it in a luggage pocket. When I arrive at the rental car lot, I place my advertising sign on the back windshield. If I'm given a car with a tinted back window that masks the sign, I place the decal on the front windshield, high enough not to block my view. This marketing approach is repeated each time I rent a car.

Anyone seeing the car on the road or parked in a lot reads the marketing message and website address. It's unclear how much the promotion has helped my business overall, as buyers rarely remember how they find a website or telephone number. But you may find yourself in a position to talk about your service in places you never considered to be a temporary office, such as malls, car washes, and ferries transporting people and cars. People will stop you in parking lots to learn about your business because of the promotional decal. This has happened to me numerous times in supermarket and mall lots. Women inquire about my services for their firms and friends who own businesses.

The sign is your business's introduction. Keep other items on hand for distribution to interested parties, such as brochures and business cards. Carry a notepad for writing names, telephone numbers, and notes about people; this will make return calls easier. Many people who talk with me neglect to carry their business cards, so I'm ready to write down the details.

One more important tip: Before you place the order, I suggest you take several days to consider the message written on your sign. An effective message or slogan must be easy to read at a glance. The decal itself only holds a specific number of letters within two rows, so long messages won't do. I chose to broadcast a three-word slogan on the top line and my website address on the bottom. It took several days to finalize my decision. I posted my ideas on an office wall to help make the right choice, and I'm still proud to place the sign in vehicles I own or rent.

This mobile promotional method effectively spreads the word about your business, and the price fits your budget because you're already on the road. We home-based and solo business owners can easily add this type of marketing to our plans.

Time to Create and Launch Your Plan

Marketing once required a team of employees to complete. That myth is finally laid to rest. You now know that the task is manageable on your own with the exception of sporadic assistance from helpers whom you direct to research, monitor, or finalize projects. Marketing techniques you select from this book will effectively put your business front and center within your chosen industry. You will implement some ideas frequently because of the high success rate each time they're launched. Other concepts introduced here may provide a promotional boost to attract a new audience. Most of all, it's up to you to create a marketing plan, revise it, and launch campaigns that bring buyers to your physical or virtual door.

In Summary

We've covered a lot of ground in this book. Here are highlights from each chapter to jumpstart your own home-based business road map.

The Marketing Plan

❑ Plan a course of action for your business success by developing a written plan.

❑ Examine area statistics, client lists (if available), current and future industry trends, and your long-range goals.

❑ Review your plan periodically to stay on track and also to change and update your goals.

Solo Marketing Basics

❑ Document all information to be placed on business cards, and double-check spellings before printing.

❑ Choose from a variety of business events, held during the day or evening, to meet like-minded people in casual environments.

❑ Meet clients at public meeting places when getting together at your home workspace is not appropriate.

Direct Mail Marketing

❑ Determine which types of printed literature make the most impact on your customers:

- ■ Letters
- ■ Postcards
- ■ Newsletters
- ■ Surveys

❏ Review junk mail and extract convincing words and powerful phrases to include in your own marketing materials.

❏ Mail handwritten appreciation notes to clients after purchases and referrals are concluded.

Print Media Marketing

❏ Create a campaign to write and distribute news releases (also known as press releases) through local and national media.

❏ Learn what the media consider newsworthy to increase your chances for coverage.

❏ Enlist the services of news release distribution services.

Broadcast Media Marketing

❏ Media options:

- General television
- Cable television
- General radio
- Satellite radio

❏ Promotion options:

- Enlist a publicist's help. Pro: Puts the work in the hands of an expert with media ties. Con: Expense may outweigh the results.
- Do it yourself. Pro: Uses your marketing skills and insight to contact specific media to reach your audience. Con: Lots of time is required, which takes you away from other business-building tasks.

❏ Media Appearance Worksheet:

- Be ready to apply your own makeup if no artist is on-site.
- For a winning appearance, wear a color other than white.
- Drink water beforehand to ensure a clean, on-camera smile; eat afterward.
- Before leaving the studio, ask the producer when to follow up by telephone for another segment.
- Write the producer an appreciation note after the broadcast.

Technology Tools

❏ Teleseminars:

- Easy to create live or as a recording on CD.
- Choose to interview another person or have someone interview you.
- Create a script to streamline the discussion.

❏ Directories:

- Make money from your expertise by creating and selling lists in text, CD, and PDF formats.
- Compile data about niche industries that would generally take hours for others to collect.

❏ Web videos:

- Promote your industry knowledge by recording and adding video clips to your website.
- Decide which online sharing community will host your videos and upload them ASAP.

❏ Web radio:

- Create an online radio show for customers who prefer to listen rather than watch videos.
- Create radio shows of no more than twenty to forty-five minutes in length.

❏ E-books:

- Decide what information to compile and create for download delivery.
- Research how to include your materials on bookstore websites for instant access after payment.

❏ Membership sites:

- Determine if you have enough resource material to start a private, online community.
- Review membership software programs and document pros and cons.

Internet Marketing

❏ Get your website up and running:

- Select a domain name and register it.
- Choose a website host with templates, e-mail addresses, blogging options, statistics program, and a secure cart to sell online.
- Review other industry websites to gauge their strengths and weaknesses.

❏ Use electronic newsletters:

- Determine your newsletter's content, frequency, and marketing options.
- Select a newsletter distribution firm that provides templates, statistics, and support.
- Monitor the newsletter's success, and continue providing information for readers.

❏ Create a website press room (also known as an online media room or "About Us" page), including:

- Description of products and services
- Product and publicity photographs
- List of media appearances
- List of publications featuring your expert quotes
- Industry background
- Celebrity and general customer endorsements/comments

Security Concerns

❏ Intellectual property that may need extra security:

- Photographs
- Articles, reports, books, and directories
- Audiotapes, videotapes, CDs, and DVDs

❏ Know which copyright, trademark, or patent products qualify for government copyright protection.

❏ Install a computer backup system to protect your data from hardware malfunctions.

Marketing with Gifts

❏ Buy gifts for clients to reward them for their loyalty and referral business.

❏ Investigate gift items at incentive shows, in magazines, and on product websites.

❏ Ensure that the gift matches the client's level of business.

Marketers' Strategy Tips

❏ Treat your product as a travel or shopping accessory for all to see.

❏ Gather and review business magazines when traveling to different regions.

❏ Promote your business with signs and decals affixed to personal vehicles and rental cars.

Above all, be creative, open to change, and willing to accept suggestions and adapt your marketing plan. Let this book be your guide to brainstorm your best ideas. Then move forward with confidence to make your marketing dreams a reality.

Index

About the Author

Shirley George Frazier is recognized world-wide as one of the foremost experts on marketing strategies for solo business owners who work without employee assistance.

As a professional speaker, Shirley is an award-winning entrepreneur who conducts seminars at worldwide conferences and trade shows; provides small business advice on CNBC, New York's Fox Channel 5, The Food Network, and the Live Well Network; publishes articles in *Gifts & Decorative Accessories*, *Spare Time Magazine*, and *Opportunities Magazine*, and is quoted in *CNN Money*, *Black Enterprise*, *Entrepreneur Magazine*, *Gift Shop Magazine*, *The Orange County Register*, *New York Newsday*, and worldwide publications. She is also author of *How to Start a Home-based Gift Basket Business* (Globe Pequot Press) and *The Gift Basket Design Book*.

Shirley lives in Paterson, New Jersey, with her daughter, Genesis, and Yorkshire Terrier twins, Mae and Pepi.